PSILOCYBIN

MAGIC MUSHROOM GROWER'S GUIDE

A Handbook for Psilocybin Enthusiasts

O.T. OSS & O.N. OERIC

Drawings by Kat
Photography by Irimias the Obscure

ISBN 9780932551061

Quick American Publishing
First Printing: November 1991

First Edition 1976
And/Or Press: 7 Printings

Revised Edition 1986
Lux Natura: 1 Printing

Layout: T. Johnson
Cover Art: Copyright 1985 by
Kathleen Harrison McKenna

DEDICATION

This book is respectfully dedicated to R. Gordon Wasson and Albert Hofmann, whose investigations of the botany and chemistry of the magic mushroom brought psilocybin to the world.

"At last you know what the ineffable is, and what ecstasy means."

—R.G. Wasson, 1972

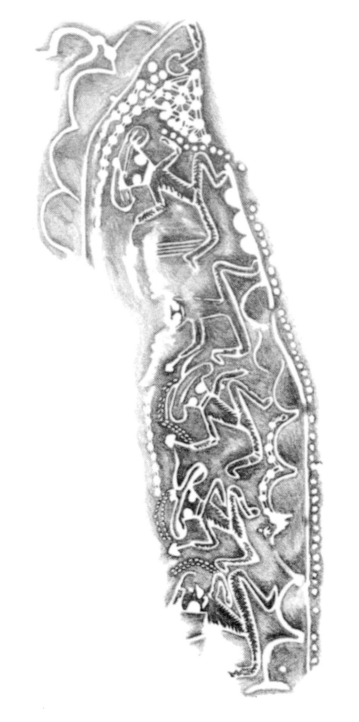

Rock painting from Tassili Plateau, Southern Algeria, circa 3500 B.C.

PREFACE TO THE REVISED EDITION

It is not often that something as fragile and culture-bound as a religious mystery can rise from the ashes of near extinction. Even the natural life of a religious mystery ends finally in erosion of connection to the mysterious driving power of some archetype. But few religious mysteries exist long enough to experience this decadence. Most are suppressed by dominant orthodoxies already in place or recently imported through conquest. This latter situation is an apt description of the status of the mushroom religion of Meso-America at the time of the Spanish Conquest.

In the case of Meso-American mushroom use, an ancient shamanic religion—of which we know next to nothing—confronted a Spanish Catholicism whose relatively advanced technology meant complete subjugation of the people, complete breakdown of the ancient gnosis. Practitioners of the mushroom cult were burned as heretics. The Indians' insistence on the mushroom as the "flesh of the gods" must have particularly excited the heretic-hunters and perhaps left them not a little uneasy as they went about their bloody business. After all, "flesh of the gods" is a claim explicitly made for the Christian Eucharist, yet it is not nearly so effective a visionary vehicle as the persecuted mushroom.

The use of the mushroom retreated to the remote mountainous peripheries of Spanish Mexico. The ritual itself was all but lost under a layer of Christianized associations. The mushrooms were called "Jesus" or "St. Peter"—their old names, names of the planetary gods of the Mayans, forgotten.

Thus the matter stood for centuries. In the 1950s Wasson made the initial discovery of the slumbering mystery, and more than two decades of mostly academic "ethnomycological" study followed. This book, first published in 1976, opened a new phase in the rebirth of the mushroom religion by placing the knowledge of cultivation into the body of publicly available information. More than a hundred thousand copies of this book have been sold, it has spawned several imitations, and it continues to sell well. This means that there are now many thousands of mushroom cultivators in the world. It is reasonable to suppose that more people are now actively involved in a religious quest using psilocybin than ever before in history. This is a complete rebirth of a religious mystery and it has taken place in less than a decade! What are the implications of this emergence of a pagan mystery into the banal world of modernity? What are its implications for those closest to this decisive, historical shift, those who, by cultivating and teaching others how to cultivate, are making the change happen?

It is clear that pharmacology intends to provide the future with an ever-expanding repertoire of psychoactive chemicals. But I wonder whether what is needed are new drugs or the courage to shamanically apply the botanical hallucinogens already sanctioned by millenia of folk usage. Few of the productions of the laboratory will be found to be as somatically benign as psilocybin or to be so structurally analogous to those compounds naturally occurring in the human brain and responsible for "normal" consciousness.

Once one has actually grown the mushroom, it becomes obvious that the mushroom uses the same strategy whether it is enveloping a petri dish or a society. A tiny part breaks away from the main body, it becomes a new center of radiative growth that expands until it reaches a critical limit, then it too spawns break-away particles with a life of their own. By this process—normally involving spores, but in cultivation involving propagation of mycelial strains, and on another level involving the teaching of cultivation techniques by one person to another—the mushroom makes its way in the world.

This implies an analogy: That knowledge of how to cultivate is spreading through society in the same way that the mycelium spreads through rye in a jar or a bed of compost. There is an apocalyptic corollary: When the technique is ubiquitous in society, "fruiting" will occur, meaning the real power and import of humanity's relationship to the mushroom will be suddenly revealed.

—Terence McKenna,
August 1985

ACE oƒ SHROOMS.

The Mixtec representation of the psychedelic experience, from the
Codex Vindobonensis Mexicanus 1.

TABLE OF CONTENTS

FOREWORD 13

INTRODUCTION 17

STEP I: Locating and Identifying the Fungus:
Collecting and Germinating Spores 22

STEP II: Growing Stock Inocula 34

STEP III: Growing on Sterilized Rye 43

STEP IV: Casing and Recasing 56

STEP V: Harvesting, Preserving, and Dosage 66

AFTERWORD 70

CONVERSION TABLE 72

CHRONOLOGY 73

BIBLIOGRAPHY 78

GLOSSARY 80

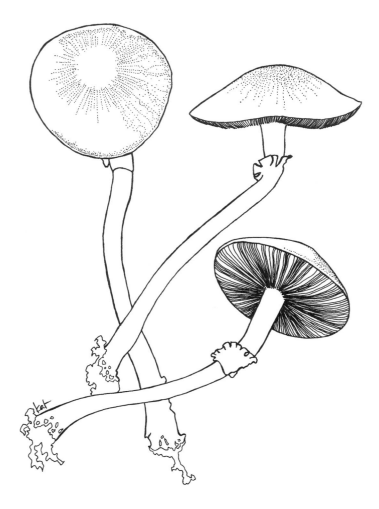

FOREWORD
by Terence McKenna

More than twenty-five years have passed since Albert Hofmann isolated and named the hallucinogen psilocybin. Hofmann's psilocybin was extracted from various species of mushrooms whose occurrence and ritual use in the mountains of Oaxaca had been discovered by Gordon and Valentina Wasson in the summer of 1953. Of the many species which were in use in Oaxaca, subsequent laboratory tests revealed that only one species was easily grown and able to fruit under a variety of artificial conditions. That one species is *Stropharia cubensis*—the starborn magic mushroom. This book is a path to this mushroom; how to grow it and how to place it in your life like the shining light that it is. The sections which follow give precise, no-fail instructions for growing and preserving the magic mushroom. We have made these instructions as clear and direct as possible; what is described is only slightly more complicated than canning or making jelly. These instructions can be adapted to undertakings of any size from a few jars to thousands.

But before all these details there should come a chat about just what this is really all about. We imagine that if you are avidly reading this book it is probably because you have taken dried mushrooms or been exposed to fresh ones in Latin America, so we do not begin with readers unfamiliar with the joys of mushroom tripping. Our instructions are a combination of research into other people's methods of cultivation and procedures which we developed, tested, and found useful ourselves. Nothing we recommend is untried by us. There may be other ways to carry on small-scale cultivation indoors but either they are variations on our method that are less direct or they are unknown to us. Cultivation of *Stropharia* outside on compost is possible in the U.S. if the local temperature is warm through the growing season. But compost cultivation is an art in itself and demands more space, more effort, and more public exposure than our indoor method. Getting involved in composting a ton of manure is not a necessary part of producing huge quantities of perfect magic mushrooms!

Our method is scientific but our opinions about *Stropharia cubensis* are not. Our opinions in this matter do not rest

13

upon the opinions of others nor upon anything written in any book, instead they rest upon the experience of five dried grams of this psilocybin mushroom; at that level a peculiar phenomenon occurs. It is the emergence of an I-Thou relationship between the person taking the psilocybin and the mental state it evokes. Jung calls this "transference" and it was a necessary condition of early and primitive humanity's relationship to its gods and demons. The mushroom speaks, and our opinions rest upon what it tells eloquently of itself in the cool night of the mind:

"I am old, older than thought in your species, which is itself fifty times older than your history. Though I have been on earth for ages I am from the stars. My home is no one planet, for many worlds scattered through the shining disc of the galaxy have conditions which allow my spores an opportunity for life. The mushroom which you see is the part of my body given to sex thrills and sun bathing, my true body is a fine network of fibers growing through the soil. These networks may cover acres and may have far more connections than the number in a human brain. My mycelial network is nearly immortal—only the sudden toxification of a planet or the explosion of its parent star can wipe me out. By means impossible to explain because of certain misconceptions in your model of reality all my mycelial networks in the galaxy are in hyperlight communication across space and time. The mycelial body is as fragile as a spider's web but the collective hypermind and memory is a vast historical archive of the career of evolving intelligence on many worlds in our spiral star swarm. Space, you see, is a vast ocean to those hardy life forms that have the ability to reproduce from spores, for spores are covered with the hardest organic substance known. Across the aeons of time and space drift many spore-forming life-forms in suspended animation for millions of years until contact is made with a suitable environment. Few such species are minded, only myself and my recently evolved near relatives have achieved the hyper-communication mode and memory capacity that makes us leading members in the community of galactic intelligence. How the hyper-communication mode operates is a secret which will not be lightly given to humans. But the means should be obvious: it is the occurence of psilocybin and psilocin in the biosynthetic pathways of my living body that opens for me and my symbiots the vision screens to many worlds.

14

You as an individual and Homo sapiens as a species are on the brink of the formation of a symbiotic relationship with my genetic material that will eventually carry humanity and earth into the galactic mainstream of the higher civilizations.

"Since it is not easy for you to recognize other varieties of intelligence around you, your most advanced theories of politics and society have advanced only as far as the notion of collectivism. But beyond the cohesion of the members of a species into a single social organism there lie richer and even more baroque evolutionary possibilities. Symbiosis is one of these. Symbiosis is a relation of mutual dependence and positive benefits for both of the species involved. Symbiotic relationships between myself and civilized forms of higher animals have been established many times and in many places throughout the long ages of my development. These relationships have been mutually useful; within my memory is the knowledge of hyper-light drive ships and how to build them. I will trade this knowledge for a free ticket to new worlds around suns younger and more stable than your own. To secure an eternal existence down the long river of cosmic time, I again and again offer this agreement to higher beings and thereby have spread throughout the galaxy over the long millenia. A mycelial network has no organs to move the world, no hands; but higher animals with manipulative abilities can become partners with the star knowledge within me and if they act in good faith, return both themselves and their humble mushroom teacher to the million worlds to which all citizens of our starswarm are heir."

15

INTRODUCTION

It seems characteristic of our condition that human beings, in whatever environmental or existential milieu they find themselves, experience an urge to seek contact with the essential mystery underlying the fact of being. Indeed, the entire odyssey of our species, both phylogenetic and historical, can be seen as a groping toward some sensed transcendent fulfillment. The story of the human race—our art, science, philosophies, civilizations and religions—is largely the story of this quest for contact with the holy, numinous, and self-transcending. It is a quest at least as old as our species; evidence indicating that early humans possessed religious consciousness has been found dating back to the Middle Paleolithic. The archeological evidence shows clearly: Human beings were at home with the concept of the sacred long before the advent of writing, agriculture, civilization, or science; it is a concept that has abided in the human imagination guiding us forward since the earliest infanthood of humanity, contemporary with and possibly preceding the earliest use of tools, fire, even language itself.

The life of pre-literate people is one in which nature exists as the primary condition of existence; one is surrounded by it, one is immersed in it, one depends upon it for one's very survival. The quest for food and for the material necessities of life must be a constant and unending one for human beings in nature, a quest in which every plant and animal that one encounters comes under the scrutiny of a restless curiosity. Given this situation, it was inevitable that sooner or later in the search for food women and men would accidentally ingest certain plants containing compounds affecting the central nervous system—and find themselves suddenly transported to a realm of the profoundest rapture and strangeness. Indeed, the ethno-mycologist R. Gordon Wasson (1958, 1961) has suggested that the accidental ingestion of an hallucinogenic plant, probably a mushroom, constituted human beings' earliest encounter with the numinosum, and led directly to the formation of the concept of deity and the supernatural. This notion is not without a certain logical appeal: it stands to reason that the restless, roving eyes of human beings, scanning nature for potential sources of food, would quickly single out the lowly mush-

17

room, so odd in appearance and so unlike the rest of the vegetation with which they were familiar. Given a few thousand years for random experimentation (a relatively short time in the scale of prehistory), they would eventually discover and ingest fungi containing centrally-active compounds, undergo the hallucinogenic experience and the connection with the numinosum would be established.

The scenario described is, of course, imaginary. We cannot know the exact circumstances under which humans first confronted the psychedelic experience. We do know, thanks to the work of Wasson and his colleagues in the 1950s (see V. P. & R.G. Wasson, 1957, R.G. Wasson & R. Heim, 1958, & Wasson, 1957), that a religious cult centered around the ritual ingestion of hallucinogenic mushrooms has existed in the highlands of central Mexico at least since before the Conquest, and is very likely much more ancient than that, its real origins having been lost in the mists of prehistoric time. But the fact remains that, whether encountered through the ingestion of a fungus or some other plant, or through some spontaneously triggered altered state of consciousness, the direct experience of the transcendent has had and is having a profound impact on human history, perhaps even on human evolution. The urge toward the transcendent—and the dynamic tension that exists between the drive to transcend and the mundane necessities which impose themselves on the primary fact of biological being—is in a sense what all history, all religion, art, philosophy, discovery and science—in short, all of human thought and civilization— is about. The urge to reach beyond the known to what is unknown and unplumbed is irredeemably woven into the fabric of human history. It is this urge which built the pyramids, Stonehenge and the Gothic cathedrals. The same urge drove frail ships across the trackless oceans to the shores of a new world, and the same urge in our own time has driven us to fling a tiny bubble of light and air across the vast and howling abysses of space (that cosmic milli-micron) that separates our earth from its moon. It is the same urge that stirs the shiver along our spines when we gaze with wonder and longing at the star-dusted sky on a clear winter's evening.

Today, we stand on the threshold of the stars. Slowly it is emerging in mass consciousness that the next evolutionary step forward will so transform humanity that all that has gone before will seem but a prelude. We stand at the edge of history ready to accelerate our human experience out into the vast chasm of night which engulfs our planet, the lessons of our historical career still echoing down the corridors of time. We are about to embark on the greatest adventure we have ever known, one that will change our very notion of what it is to be human; yet we should not forget that between ourselves as we ascend the ramp of the starship and our mushroom munching ancestor gazing into his Paleolithic fire lie only seconds of cosmic time.

This book is essentially a how-to manual for those who have the interest, time, and patience required for cultivating "the magic mushroom" in their own homes. It is for people who feel that they still may be able to learn something by experiencing the primordial visions of their ancestors, and feel it strongly enough that they are willing to invest a little time, money and effort in order to realize that vision. By "magic mushroom" is meant those mushrooms which are members of the genus *Psilocybe*, and the closely related genera *Stropharia, Conocybe, Panaeolus,* and *Copelandia*. Certain members of these genera contain the compounds psilocybin (4-phosphoryloxy-N,N-dimethyltryptamine) and psilocin (4-hydroxy-N,N-dimethyltryptamine) as the active hallucinogenic agents (fig. 1). These compounds contain the basic indole structure characteristic of most hallucinogens found in nature (see Schultes, 1973, p. 17 ff.), including various amides of lysergic acid (of which LSD is a semisynthetic representative), N,N-dimethyltryptamine, harmine and its analogues, and ibogaine. The most notable exception to this basic structure is mescaline, which chemically is 3,4,5-trimethoxyphenylethylamine, and hence is in the same class as amphetamine (a-methylphenyl-ethylamine).

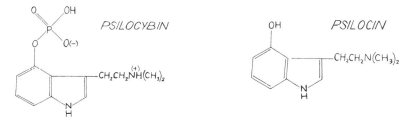

fig. 1: Structural formulas for psilocybin and psilocin.

19

The cultivation information in this book pertains only to one species of magic mushroom, *Stropharia cubensis* Earle. (The mycologist Rolf Singer has recently reclassified this species into the genus *Psilocybe*. Hence in some references it is referred to as *Psilocybe cubensis* Earle ex. Singer.) It is probable that with appropriate adaptations the methods outlined here could be applied successfully to the cultivation of other species. Our experience has shown, however, that *Stropharia cubensis* is the easiest to cultivate. Those interested in the cultivation of other mushroom species should consult *The Mushroom Cultivator* by Stamets and Chilton, published by Agarikon Press, Olympia, Washington, 1983. Our limiting the discussion to one species, however, is not as unfortunate as it may seem since *Stropharia cubensis* is not only one of the strongest of the hallucinogenic mushrooms, but also one of the most widespread and readily obtainable. In nature, its habitat is cowdung, and it can be found in pastures during rainy, warm parts of the year in regions as diverse as the Southeastern U.S. and Cambodia, Australia and Colombia. Unlike other psilocybin-containing genera, which with few exceptions are fairly restricted endemics, the distribution of the *Stropharia cubensis* is world-wide (Pollock, 1975). In fact, since its preferred habitat is cow-dung, its circumtropical distribution has doubtless been encouraged, if not caused, by the world cattle industry. Amusingly enough, the *Stropharia* could be said to exist as a "weed" on high-technology cattle-raising cultures. This intimate association with humans via domesticated cattle has probably existed for as long as humanity has possessed pastoral technology.

The procedures outlined in this book, if followed with care and persistence, will work for *Stropharia cubensis*. The procedures can be carried out by anyone in their own home, with just a minimum of equipment and a few supplies and common chemicals that are no more than moderately difficult to obtain. No special training in mycology or microbiology is necessary. What is necessary is to follow the instructions closely and carefully.

The procedure described herein consists essentially of four major steps. It begins with spores and describes step-by-step instructions for growing full-size mushrooms from spores within six weeks. The first step involves locating the fungus, collecting and germinating the spores, and isolating the mycelium, or fungal threads, obtained

20

from the spores. The next step involves cultivating the mycelium on agar, a solid nutrient, in order to use it for inoculation. In the third step, mycelium grown on agar is then grown on a sterilized medium of whole rye grains. In the fourth and final step the rye-grown mycelium is *cased*, or covered with soil, a process that induces the production of mushrooms. This book describes each of these steps in detail, and can be put into practice by anyone able to read and carefully follow the instructions, provided that they can obtain spores or specimens of *Stropharia cubensis*.

STEP 1:
LOCATING AND IDENTIFYING THE FUNGUS:
COLLECTING AND GERMINATING SPORES

In the New World, *Stropharia cubensis* can be found in appropriate habitats throughout the Southern U.S., all through the coastal regions of Mexico, and throughout coastal and equatorial regions of South America. In the U.S., it has been reported from Texas, Louisiana, Alabama, Mississippi, Arkansas, Florida, Tennessee, and Georgia. Its distribution would probably be even greater were it not for the fact that its environmental requirements limit it to regions of mild temperatures and high humidity.

Because of its specific habitat and singular appearance, *Stropharia cubensis* is one of the easiest mushrooms to locate and identify. As already mentioned, it can be found growing out of cow-pies in pastures during rainy warm seasons. Other dung-growing mushrooms may also be found in the same pasture, but these bear little resemblance to *Stropharia*. The following botanical description of *Stropharia cubensis* is taken from *Mushrooms of North America* by Orson K. Miller, Jr.:

> Cap pale yellowish, viscid; persistent ring; blue-staining stalk.
> Cap 1.5-8 cm broad, conic, bell-shaped, convex in age, viscid, without hairs, whitish to pale yellow, light brownish in age, stains bluish in age. Flesh firm, white, bruises blue. Gills adnate (attached) to adnexed (notched), close, grey to violet-grey in age with white edges. Stalk 4-15 mc long, 4-14 mm thick, enlarging somewhat toward the base, dry, without hairs, white staining blue when bruised. Veil white, leaving a superior membranous ring. Spores 10-17μ x 7-10μ elliptical to oval in side-view, thick-walled, with a large pore at apex, purple-brown spore print. Cystidia (sterile cells) on gill edge club-shaped with rounded heads.

Miller places this species in the genus *Psilocybe*, after Singer.
The flesh of this mushroom exhibits the property of staining a bluish color when bruised or broken. This blue-

22

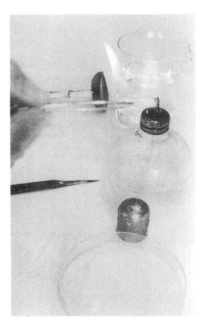 

fig. 2: Sterilizing the slide.   **fig. 3**: Decapitation

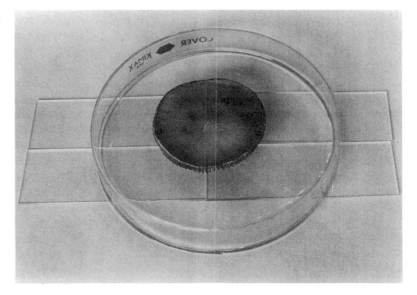

fig. 4: Making spore print (note slide arrangement).

24

staining reaction is apparently an enzymatic oxidation of psilocin to an indole diquinone (Bocks, 1967) and is a fairly reliable indicator of the presence of psilocybin, not only in *Stropharia cubensis*, but also in other closely related genera (members of the family Strophariaceae) (cf. Benedict, et al., 1967). Other mushrooms, such as members of the genus *Russula*, section Nigricantinae, and *Boletus*, exhibit a similar blueing. The blueing in these cases, however, is not due to the presence of indole substrates and these mushrooms otherwise bear no resemblance whatever to *Stropharia cubensis* or related species (Singer, 1958, p. 247).

Once one has located a specimen or specimens of *Stropharia cubensis*, and been satisfied as to its identity in all particulars, it is necessary to collect spores for cultivation. Spores can be easily collected in the following manner: Take one or more fresh specimens with the caps fully open; using a sharp knife, cut off the stipe as close to the gills as possible (see fig. 3) and place the cap gillside down on a clean sheet of white paper, and leave for 24 hours. It doesn't hurt to cover the caps with a small bowl while taking the spore print in order to prevent dessication. When the caps are removed, a dark-purplish, radially symmetrical deposit of spores will remain on the paper where the gills contacted it. The paper should then be folded and sealed in an envelope in order to prevent further contamination by airborne spores of other species of lower fungi. A single spore-print contains tens of millions of spores, and is sufficient to make hundreds of spore germinations.

The following variation on this method was suggested to us as a way of enhancing the sterility of the spore print: Take four standard flat microscope slides, swab with alcohol, and flame in an alcohol flame or butane torch (fig. 2). On a clean flat surface, such as a table-top swabbed with Lysol, lay the slides side by side and end to end, so that they are arranged as in fig. 3. Place the fresh cap in the exact middle of the slides so that approximately ¼ of the cap covers each slide (fig. 4). Cover and wait 24 hours. When the cap is removed, the end of each slide will be covered with spores, and the slides can then be sealed, together or separately, in plastic or paper. One can easily substitute glass microscope coverslips for the slides to maximize compactness. Do not use plastic coverslips, since static electricity associated with them makes it difficult for the spores to adhere to them.

Once the spore-print has been collected, it is necessary to germinate some spores in order to begin the life cycle that will eventually culminate in the production of more mushrooms. Before we outline procedures for germinating the spores, a brief discussion of the stages in the life cycle of these higher fungi follows; readers who do not care to read this somewhat technical portion may skip the next three paragraphs.

All gilled fungi are members of the class Basidiomycetes, i.e., they are characterized by the production of spores on club-shaped appendages called *basidia*. Spores borne on basidia are called *basidiospores*. Most of the conspicuous fungi that one encounters, such as mushrooms, puffballs, and bracket fungi are members of the subclass Homobasidiomycetes. Of the members of this subclass, the gilled mushrooms are placed in the order Agaricales. The life cycle of a typical homobasidiomycete is illustrated on the facing page. The basidiospores germinate to form a monokaryotic hypha. A hypha is a tubular filament; an aggregation of these hyphae collectively comprise a mass of thread-like filaments referred to as the *mycelium*. The mycelium comprises the main body, or *thallus*, of the fungus. The stalked, capped structure which we call the mushroom is actually only the "fruiting body" or the spore-producing reproductive structure, and constitutes only a small portion of the total mass of the fungus; the great bulk of the organism exists underground in the form of a network of mycelium, which occasionally "fruits," or produces mushrooms, under appropriate conditions.

The basidiospores germinate to produce a *monokaryotic* mycelium, i.e., a mycelium having only one nucleus per cell. This mycelium grows out until it encounters another monokaryotic mycelium, germinated from another spore, that is a compatible mating type. If the monokaryotic mycelium does not contact a compatible monokaryotic mycelium, it eventually dies. In situations where two compatible monokaryotic mycelia do make contact, however, a process called *somatogamy*, or the fusing of the somatic cells of the two mycelia, takes place, *but fusion of the nuclei does not take place*. The result of somatogamy is the establishment of a *dikaryotic* mycelium, i.e., a mycelium possessing two nuclei, one from each of the monokaryotic mycelia, in each of its cells (see facing page). The dikary-

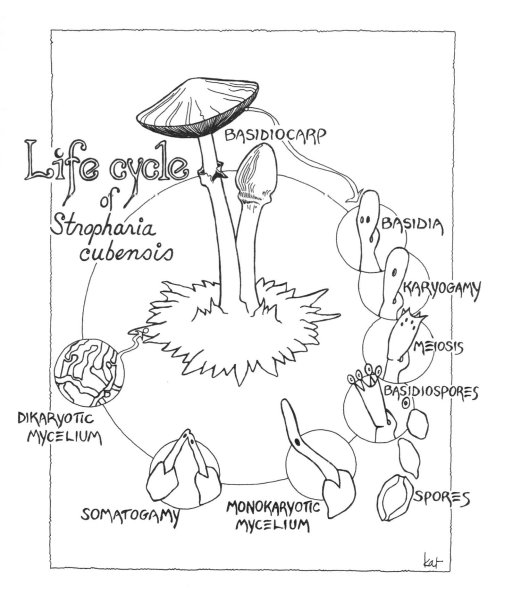

otic mycelium stage is the most prolonged portion of the life cycle and is also the main assimilative stage of the fungus. The dikaryotic mycelium can propagate vegetatively indefinitely without going through a sexual (spore-producing) stage. Given appropriate conditions, however, the dikaryotic mycelium can be induced to "fruit": the undifferentiated mycelial thallus of the fungus begins to weave itself together into an articulated, spore-bearing "fruiting body," in this case, into a mushroom. The mushroom continues to enlarge and thrust above the ground, incorporating more and more mycelium while at the same time expanding by absorption of water. At a certain stage in the growth of the mushroom, or *basidiocarp*, club-shaped structures called *basidia* form on the underside of the gills. At this point, *karyogamy*, or fusion of the two nuclei of the dikaryotic mycelium takes place within the basidia (see preceding page). This is the only *diploid*, or 2n, stage in the life-cycle of the fungus, and is also the briefest stage, for meiosis, or reduction division of a diploid (2n) nucleus to 4 haploid (n) nuclei occurs immediately following karyogamy. The result of meiosis is the production of four haploid nuclei within the basidium; these are then pushed out of the basidium and become surrounded by hard sheaths to form the basidiospores. The result is the basidium bearing four basidiospores on its outer surface as in the "Life Cycle" drawing. These basidiospores eventually detach from the basidium to begin the life cycle again.

Fungi of the family Strophariaceae, which includes *Stropharia cubensis* and most other psilocybin-containing genera, are genetically complex with respect to the mating compatibility of different monokaryotic mycelia. These fungi are *heterothallic* and *tetrapolar*, that is, their sexual cycle is dependent on the fusion of two compatible monokaryotic mycelia, and their sexual compatibility is governed by two sets of factors:

> In tetrapolar heterothallism, two sets of factors, the A's and B's, are involved. If a sexually reproducing thallus is to be established, somatogamy must occur between mycelia differing in both sets of factors—for example AB x ab. The number of mating classes is somewhat greater than in bipolar forms, since four types typically arise from spores of a single basidiocarp. Obviously these mating types, numbering in the hundreds in both bipolar and tetrapolar species, cannot be designated as sexes! (Scagel, et al., 1967, p. 69.)

Keeping this information pertaining to the sexual characteristics of these fungi in mind, let us return to the problem of spore germination; the relevance of our digression into the matter of life cycle and sexual compatibility will be seen shortly.

Once one has obtained a spore print from *Stropharia cubensis*, the monokaryotic mycelium can be easily obtained by germinating the spores on an appropriate solid nutrient medium, such as Potato Dextrose Agar or Malt Extract Agar. A more detailed discussion of various kinds of nutrient agars and how to prepare them will be given below in the section of Growing Stock Inocula. For the present, however, simply assume that one has several clean, sterile petri plates which have been filled with an appropriate solid nutrient medium (see fig. 5). Spores car be transferred most readily using a clean, sterile #11 scalpel, inoculating loop, or similar instrument. Flame the blade of the scalpel in an alcohol flame, then reach into the petri dish and cut a small square of agar (2-3 mm²) from the center of the dish. Spear the agar square on the blade of the scalpel, and use it to lightly touch the surface of the paper or slide on which the spore-print is deposited. Replace the agar square on the medium close to the place it was cut. It is sometimes convenient to inoculate four agar squares in each dish, one in each quadrant. Care should be taken to do this as quickly as possible, keeping the cover off the petri plate for the shortest time necessary, in order to minimize the chances of contaminating the plate with the airborne spores of contaminants. A variation on this method can also be used: Instead of scraping the spores directly onto the plate, they can first be scraped into about 10 ml of sterilized water. Shake this vigorously, then dilute to 100 ml by adding sterile water. Using a sterilized pipette or syringe, take up 2-3 ml of diluted spore solution, and point-inoculate the petri plate by placing a drop of the solution at two or three separate points on the plate.

If possible, incubate the covered inoculated plate at 86 degrees F. for 24 to 36 hours. This will break dormancy and force the spores to germinate faster. Spores will germinate without this incubation, but may take up to 24 days. During this time, the spores will germinate and monokaryotic mycelium will grow radially outward from each point of inoculation. The plate should be left undis-

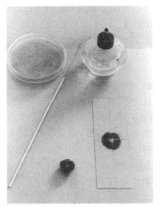

fig. 5: Completed spore print and inoculating equipment.

fig. 6: Flaming the inoculating loop.

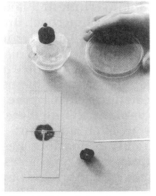

fig. 7: Touching inoculating loop to spore print.

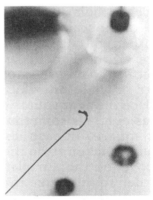

fig. 8: Hooked inoculating loop with adhering spores.

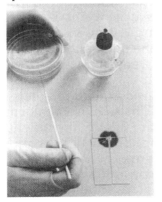

fig. 9: Inoculating petri plate with spores.

turbed until the mycelia from two different spores or two different points of inoculation have grown together and made contact. A few days after contact has occurred, one can be reasonably sure that somatogamy has taken place and that a dikaryotic mycelium has been established. Since in practice one transfers clumps of spores rather than single spores onto the plate, waiting for two different inoculation spots to make contact is not really essential; by the time mycelial growth is well established on the plate, one can be confident of isolating dikaryotic mycelium.

In cultivating the fungus to the fruiting stage, one works primarily with a single strain of dikaryotic mycelium. However, because spores of several different mating types are produced by a single mushroom, a petri plate inoculated with spores will have possibly several dozen different strains of dikaryotic mycelium growing on it. It is therefore necessary to isolate one of the strains so that one can grow out stock inocula from a single, uniform strain. This can be accomplished using a scalpel, dissecting needle or inoculating loop in which the loop has been bent to form a hook (fig. 8). The implement is first sterilized in an alcohol flame; then the petri plate is opened slightly and a very small piece of mycelial tissue is snagged on the end of the blade, needle, or hook, and transferred rapidly and deftly to a second clean sterile petri plate containing an appropriate solid nutrient medium. Dikaryotic mycelium is isolated using exactly the same techniques as are used in transferring mycelium from one petri plate to another; for figures illustrating this procedure, see Step II, figs. 13-16. By selecting a very small piece of tissue in this way, one can be reasonably sure that only one strain of dikaryotic mycelium is being removed and isolated. In practice we find that both isolation of a dikaryon and plate-to-plate transfer of dikaryotic mycelium once isolated, can be most easily accomplished using a sterile #11 scalpel. Small agar squares can be cut from the edge of the mycelial thallus and transferred to fresh petri dishes.

The dikaryotic mycelium thus isolated from the spore-germination plate will grow outward in all directions from the point of inoculation on the new plate and should cover most of the surface of the medium within 8-12 days. One can then go ahead and make further transfers to new plates with a fair degree of certainty that one is working with a single strain of dikaryotic mycelium.

It is probably advisable to isolate several different strains of dikaryotic mycelium onto separate plates by taking tissue from different sections of the spore-germination plate. Different strains isolated from a single spore-germination plate should be identified by labels and compared for vigor of growth and vigor of fruiting ability, so that, through observation and trial-and-error, the strain showing maximum vigor in both respects can eventually be identified and used exclusively thereafter. Isolating the most vigorous strain takes time and careful observation; however, this need not interfere with continuing on to the second and third steps of the process, since *any* dikaryotic mycelium that has been properly isolated from other strains should exhibit fruiting ability. After several strains have been put through several fruiting stages it should be apparent which strain is most vigorous. Our observations indicate that the most vigorous fruiting strains have a distinctly "ropy" morphology when growing in the mycelial stage. This stands to reason, since this ropy appearance is due to the formation of *rhizoids*, thick strands of hyphae, which are similar in structure to the rhizoids formed prior to and during the fruiting stage. Those rhizoids function in the transport of water and nutrients to the developing mushrooms (see Chang & Hayes, 1978, Chapter 8).

If one has fresh mushroom specimens, it is possible to employ another method of isolating dikaryotic mycelium without utilizing spores. This is the method of subcutaneous isolation (Enos, 1970). The operation should be performed with clean hands and implements. A pair of latex gloves sterilized by spraying with Lysol should be worn. Hold the fresh mushrooms by the stipe in one hand, and with the other hand swab the cap surface lightly with a sterile cotton swab dampened with tincture of iodine. Have ready a clean #11 scapel and an alcohol lamp to sterilize it. Grasp the cap of the mushroom, top up, between the thumb and fingers until it splits open to reveal the interior whitish flesh. Flame the scapel and remove a small piece of this subcutaneous flesh and transfer it to a sterilized nutrient plate. Several inoculations can be made from the interior flesh of a single cap. Since the flesh of the mushroom has been woven together out of dikaryotic mycelium, it will grow out across the plate in the same manner as mycelium isolated from a spore-germination plate. This procedure eliminates the step of having to isolate different dikaryotic strains, since mycelium isolated in this manner consists of only one strain. On the other hand, this procedure limits one to working with only one strain.

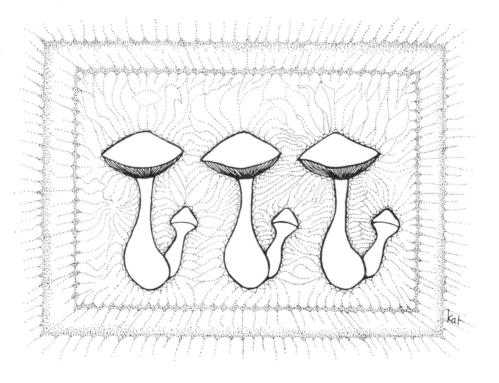

STEP II:
GROWING STOCK INOCULA

Once one or more strains of dikaryotic mycelia have been successfully isolated, it is necessary to build up a stock of mycelial cultures grown on sterile agar media. The inocula from this stock will be used to inoculate the mycelium onto sterilized rye or other grain. Before proceeding to this step, however, it is advisable to have a good supply of inocula grown out of sterile agar media, so that one will have plenty of sterile inocula even if a few cultures should succumb to contamination. The information in this section therefore describes procedures for preparation, sterilization, and inoculation of solid nutrient media.

Most laboratory work with higher fungi, yeasts, molds, bacteria and so on involves growing the organism on a solid *agar* medium to which appropriate nutrients have been added. Agar is a pectin-like substance extracted from certain kinds of sea-kelp, which, when dissolved in boiling water and allowed to cool, solidifies to a gelatinous consistency. Agar is a standard item in all microbiological work, and is available from almost any scientific supply company. It is also stocked by many health-food stores and Oriental food stores as a dietary supplement. Fungi Perfecti (P.O. Box 7634, Olympia, WA 98507) offers a wide variety of mushroom-growing supplies and will send you a very helpful catalog for $2.50.

Potato Dextrose Agar (PDA) and Malt Extract Agar (MEA) are standard nutrient media suitable for cultivating the mycelia of most higher fungi, including *Stropharia cubensis*. Both types are commonly available in a premixed form from most scientific supply companies. The premixed type need only be dissolved in boiling distilled water. Usually about 15-20 g of pre-mixed agar medium per 1000 ml of water is used.

The appropriate proportions and mixing instructions are usually printed on the container of dried agar preparation. With very little trouble, one can also manufacture one's own PDA or MEA. Recipes for PDA, MEA, and a variation of MEA called MYP for Malt-Yeast-Peptone are given below. We have found MYP to be excellent for long term maintenance of vigorous mycelium.

34

P.D.A.

250 g potatoes
15 g agar
10 g dextrose
1.5 g nutritional yeast (or yeast extract)

Shred the unpeeled potatoes into a colander and then rinse them for thirty seconds with cold tap water. Combine the rinsed potatoes with one liter of water and gently boil for thirty minutes. Filter the resulting potato broth through muslin or cheesecloth and discard the potatoes. To the liter of potato broth add the agar, dextrose, and yeast which you have previously weighed out and mixed together in a baggie. While stirring gently add in the mixed powdered ingredients. Gently boil for ten minutes or until the solution is clear. Take care not to allow the solution to boil over. Add enough water to return the total volume of the solution to one liter. Pour the solution while still hot into petri plates, baby food jars, or slant culture tubes (fig. 11). Use just enough to cover the bottom of a plate or baby-food jar to a depth of about ¼ inch full. For convenience, the plates may first be placed in the bottom of the cooker before the medium is poured; then pour the medium, put the covers on the plates, then build a second stack on top of that; then pour, cover, and stack again, until a stack similar to fig. 12 has been built. The solution may be allowed to cool or sterilized immediately. Sterilization procedures will be described shortly.

A recipe for Malt Extract Agar (MEA) follows.

To 1 liter of gently boiling water add a previously weighed and mixed powder containing:

20 g malt or malt extract (may be powder or syrup)
25 g agar
0.1 g potassium dibasic (K_2HPO)
0.1 g calcium carbonate ($CaCO_3$) (powdered oyster
    shell may be used)

The liquid malt extract sold in the syrup sections of most grocery stores is quite suitable for this medium. After the nutrients have been completely dissolved in the water, the hot solution is poured into plates in the same manner as the PDA.

MYP or Malt-Yeast-Peptone medium is a variation on MEA very useful for long term maintenance of desirable cultures. To 1 liter of gently boiling water add a previously weighed and mixed powder containing:

7 g malt extract (powder or syrup)
1 g peptone or sytone
0.5 g yeast extract
15 g agar

Soytone and Peptone are commercial brands of a protein hydrolysate and can be purchased from scientific or micro-biological supply houses.

In the case of all three of these recipes, if some of the nutrient solution is left over after pouring the plates, the flask may be sealed and stored in the refrigerator indefinitely, or sterilized with the plates and stored on the shelf. When one wishes to make more plates, the medium can be reliquified over heat and reused.

The three types of media described above are quite easy to prepare and will be suitable for growing stock inocula. It is a good idea to mix up and have on hand at least two types of media, and to use them alternately in preparing batches of plates. In this way the fungus will not become accustomed to one type of medium and thus will be forced to use different parts of its genome in adapting to the different media. This will prevent the mycelium from succumbing to any "senescence factor" or tendency to age physiologically and thus to lose vigor after a period of time.

These three types of media are completely adequate for growing out one's stock inocula. From a purely practical standpoint, we have found them to be easily and readily prepared from a relatively few common ingredients. Unless one wishes to get involved in complex nutritional studies, it is unnecessary to bother with other recipes. Other types of media may be used, however, and those who do wish to get more deeply into this step of the process are urged to consult Neal, et. al. (1968).

36

Once one has prepared an agar medium and poured it into the petri plates, baby food jars, slant culture tubes, or other suitable receptacles, it is necessary to sterilize the medium in the receptacles in order to kill the spores of bacteria, yeasts, and other molds which get into the medium from the air. This can be done via the following procedure: If a laboratory autoclave is not available, a standard home cooking or canning pressure cooker can be used. We use and recommend the All American 941½ pressure cooker, available from its manufacturer, The American Aluminum Foundry Co., P.O. Box 246, Manitowoc, Wisconsin 54220 (see fig. 27). Place a small amount of water (approx. 1 liter) in the bottom of the cooker (tap water will do) so that the surface is covered. Place the receptacles containing the medium into the pressure cooker. Be sure to stack them carefully (see fig. 12); a small enameled tray is useful for this. Note: If using pre-sterilized plastic plates, pour the medium into the plates *after* sterilizing; *do not autoclave plastic plates.*

It does not matter whether the medium is still hot and liquid, or whether it has been allowed to cool and solidify, since the heat of the sterilization process will reliquify the medium anyway. If baby food jars or culture tubes are used, *be certain that the lids are left loose, not screwed down tight,* when they are being sterilized. Seal the lid of the pressure cooker, *but leave the stopcock open.* Bring the cooker to a boil over high heat on a stove. When the water has begun to boil vigorously, a good head of steam will begin to vent through the stopcock; it should be closed at this point, and the pressure allowed to build up to between 15-20 lbs. Then reduce the heat just enough to maintain pressure at this level for 45 minutes to 1 hour. The standard sterilization time for solid media at these temperatures (250 degrees F.) and pressures (15-20 lbs.) is 15 minutes, but experience has shown that this is often insufficient to insure complete sterilization. Allowing a visible head of steam to build up in the pressure cooker before closing the stopcock is also important, for if it is closed prematurely, the pressure will rise but the water will be unable to vaporize, and dry heat requires much longer to accomplish sterilization.

After the medium has been sterilized at the correct pressure for 45-60 minutes, turn off the heat or carefully remove the cooker (remember that the medium is liquid

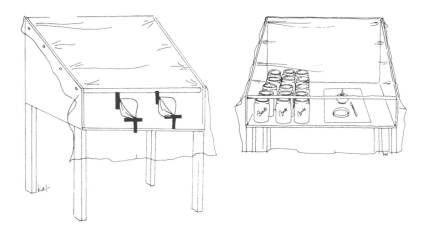

fig. 10: Two views of a homemade inoculating hood.

at this point and can slosh around) and allow the cooker to cool to room temperature *before opening the stopcock*; otherwise, the sudden release of pressure will cause the medium to boil over.

When the cooker has cooled to room temperature or slightly above, wrap the column of the stopcock with an inch wide piece of paper toweling, then dampen it with an aerosol Lysol spray and then open the stopcock and allow any excess steam to escape. Remove the lid and carefully remove the receptacles containing the medium. Place the receptacles inside a pre-sterilized inoculating hood (see fig. 10) or on a clean, smooth tabletop which has been wiped down with Lysol or similar strong disinfectant. As the receptacles cool further, the medium will solidify. If

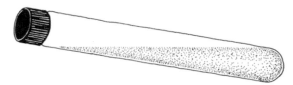

slant culture tubes are being used, they should be placed on an angle while the medium is still liquid, to provide maximum surface area for mycelial growth.

Note: PLASTIC PLATES CANNOT BE AUTOCLAVED! If using pre-sterilized plastic petri plates, the medium should be sterilized in a flask sealed with tinfoil. The flask should be about ½ full, so it is best to sterilize two 1000 ml flasks with 500 ml each of medium. The procedure for pouring plastic plates is described below.

If pre-sterilized plastic plates are being used, one proceeds as follows: Allow the sterilized flasks to cool in the inoculating hood until they are warm to the touch, but can be handled easily. The medium is still liquid at this point, and is ready to be poured. Working with the usual sterile precautions (see below), one requires an alcohol flame and a stack of 20-40 plastic petri plates. These commonly come packaged in rolls of twenty. Begin with a stack of about five plates. Carefully peel back the tinfoil from the lip of the flask of medium, and flame the flask lip briefly in the alcohol flame. Then, holding the flask in one hand, with the other carefully lift the lid from the bottom plate in the stack, keeping the other plates balanced on top of it. Hold the lip of the flask close to the edge of the petri plate. Pour just enough medium to cover the bottom of the plate to a depth of about ¼ inch. Carefully replace the cover and then repeat the process with the next lowest plate and so on up the stack. After the plates have been poured, they should be stacked (carefully!) in columns of 10 or 20 in order to minimize condensation on the lids while cooling.

When the receptacles have cooled completely to room temperature, and the medium is fully solidified, they are ready to be inoculated. If possible, inoculation should be carried out inside an inoculation hood such as that shown in fig. 10. Commercial hoods are available, or a homemade hood can be constructed out of wood and all joints sealed with silicon caulking compound. Pre-sterilize the hood before introducing the culture receptacles by spraying all inside surfaces thoroughly with Lysol aerosol, or a mixture of 25% Clorox-distilled water solution, or both. If a hood is not available, inoculation can be carried out in the open air in a room in which the air is relatively still, i.e., a room without any drafts. The air of the room should be sprayed beforehand with 25% Clorox solution and the surface on which inoculation is to be done wiped down with a strong Lysol solution. All sterile procedures should always be done wearing latex gloves which have been sterilized by spraying with Lysol (figs. 13 & 14). Never use aerosol Lysol spray in the presence of any flame. After spraying Lysol in the inoculating hood, wait a few minutes before introducing the alcohol lamp into the hood. *REMEMBER THAT SPRAY LYSOL IS HIGHLY FLAMMABLE.*

Inoculation should be done using a disposable scalpel or an inoculating loop which has been opened to form a hook (fig. 8), and can be carried out in essentially the same manner as was described for isolating dikaryotic mycelium from a spore germination plate. Select a completely sterile, vigorously growing culture from one's stock of dikaryotic mycelium isolated from spores. The mycelium of a vigorous culture should be pure white and ropey in appearance, and preferably less than 10 days old (cf. fig. 13). Wash one's hands and arms thoroughly in soap and water before beginning work, then wipe down with alcohol. Wear thin latex gloves sprayed with Lysol or Clorox-water solution as added protection (figs. 13 & 14); talcum powder can be sprinkled inside first to make them easy to slip on. Wear a short-sleeved or sleeveless shirt for the process to avoid introducing contaminants from one's clothes. Pass the scalpel or hooked inoculating loop through the flame of an alcohol lamp until the working tip has been heated to redness (fig. 15). Allow it to cool for a moment or quench it in a petri dish of sterilized agar sacrificed to this purpose. Open the culture just enough to insert the end of the loop, and snag a small piece of mycelial tissue or small plug of agar and transfer this rapidly to the freshly sterilized medium, again opening the lid just enough to insert the inoculum (fig. 16). Withdraw the loop and replace the lid on the newly inoculated culture. If a scalpel is used instead of a loop, inoculation can be accomplished by cutting a small square (1 sq. mm) of mycelia-grown agar from the culture plate, and transferring this to the new plate. If using tubes or baby food jars, the lids should be left fairly loose to allow for aeration. Repeat this process for as many times as one has receptacles to inoculate. It is not necessary to use a new culture for each inoculation; a single culture is sufficient to inoculate dozens of fresh plates. After a batch has been inoculated, however, the culture used as the source of inocula should be discarded.

Let the freshly inoculated medium stand at room temperature for 3-5 days. During this time the pure white, thread-like mycelium will spread radially across the surface of the medium, covering it completely within 7-20 days. Growth of the inoculum should be apparent by the fourth day after inoculation. Also apparent by about this time will be any contaminants that have gotten into the

fig. 11: Three containers suitable for agar culture.

fig. 12: A simple stable stack of petri plates.

fig. 13: Materials for plate-to-plate inoculation.

fig. 14: Disinfecting rubber gloves with Lysol.

fig. 15: Flaming the inoculating scalpel.

fig. 16: Inserting inoculum in fresh petri plate.

cultures during inoculation in spite of precautions. They usually appear as small white dots with blue-green centers, and grow much more rapidly than the mycelium. These are usually other molds, such as Penicillium and Aspergillus, Neurospora or various yeasts. Most are easy to distinguish from the mushroom mycelium, since the mycelium is pure white, occasionally with a slight tinge of blue, while the contaminants may be green, blue-green, black, yellow, dirty-gray, and so on, and otherwise do not resemble the mycelium. Any contaminated cultures should be discarded as soon as one is certain that contamination is present. It is normal to lose a few cultures to contamination, and one should not be discouraged by it. It is practically impossible, under non-laboratory conditions, to eliminate all contamination; but as one gains practice in making inoculations, speed and technique should gradually improve so that contamination can be held to a minimum. It would be a good idea to consult an introductory microbiology text for information relating to fast and efficient inoculating techniques.

After the plates have been inoculated, they may be stored while growing out in a sealed styrofoam box or cake box which has been sterilized by washing out with strong Clorox solution, then sprayed on all inside surfaces with Lysol. This will help to prevent contamination during growth. In very humid climates, water will condense on the tops of the plates; sometimes this can drip down on the surface of the agar and contaminate it. For this reason one should try to use only plates in which condensation is minimal, to avoid introducing unseen contaminants into the jars or rye; or, if plates with condensation are used, one should be very careful, while inoculating, to avoid knocking drops of water onto the agar surface when removing and replacing the cover. We have found that regardless of what type of plates are used, condensation on the cover can be eliminated by stacking the plates in taller (and more precarious) stacks of fifteen or more during the cooling down of the media.

STEP III:
GROWING ON STERILIZED RYE

When a number of mycelial cultures have been successfully grown on solid agar medium, one is faced with a choice: It is possible to stop at this point, and concentrate on perfecting techniques for mycelial growth on agar. The mycelium itself contains psilocybin and can be ingested for hallucinogenic effects. The amount of psilocybin present in the mycelium is determined by the richness of the medium on which it is grown. Thus for an individual wishing only to obtain psilocybin from mycelium, there is a wide-open area for investigation; viz., to discover a suitable nutrient medium that gives a maximum yield of psilocybin per unit surface area of agar. If laboratory facilities are available, psilocybin can also be obtained from mycelium grown in liquid medium in shaken or submerged flask cultures. Since the necessary equipment for this is unavailable to most people, this approach is not discussed further here. Interested readers are urged to consult Catalfomo & Tyler, 1964.

The other choice at this stage involves moving on to the third step in the procedure, whereby mushrooms can be obtained by inducing the mycelium to fruit. In order for vigorous fruiting to take place, the mycelium must first be grown out onto sterilized rye, wheat, barley or other similar grain, so that a mass of mycelium weighing from 50-100 grams is obtained. The growing of mushroom mycelium on sterilized grain is a standard procedure in commercial mushroom culture that is used to produce "spawn" for inoculation into beds of horse-manure compost. The procedures described in this section are in fact adapted, with appropriate modifications, from a process originally developed by San Antonio (1971) for growing fruits of the common edible mushroom *Agaricus bisporus* under laboratory conditions. The steps involved in growing the mycelium onto rye-grain medium are described below.

While the mycelium will grow and fruit suitably on many types of grain, including rye, wheat, barley, triticale, oats, brown rice, sorghum, millet and even buckwheat, our experience is that rye works as good as any and is less expensive than most. Therefore we have primarily worked with rye in this stage. One must be certain, however, that the rye used is packaged for human consumption, and not grown as feed; feed rye has usually been treated with a fungicide.

At this stage, it is useful to construct a styrofoam box with a window in the lid such as illustrated in figs. 17-20. These boxes can be obtained from pet stores and tropical fish dealers and can be used as a convenient modular system for incubating jars in a high-humidity, constant temperature environment. Jars may also be kept in an aquarium or a terrarium of suitable size. Such a case may be outfitted with a Grow-lux light and a timer set to a 13-hour light cycle to provide a nearly perfect growth environment. If one is working in an environment where temperature fluctuations are minimal and conditions are clean, the jars can simply be incubated on a shelf or table without any special containers.

To prepare the rye medium, begin with a clean, wide-mouth quart Mason jar with a dome and ring lid. Add the following ingredients to the jar in these proportions:

160 ml rye berries (dry weight approx 150 g)
130 ml water (tap or distilled)
½ tsp. of calcium carbonate (CaCO$_3$)

The calcium carbonate, which is optional, need not be of great purity; powdered oyster shell, powdered limestone, or powdered chalk is suitable.

When the ingredients have been added to each jar in the proper proportions, the lids should be screwed *loosely* onto the jars, *with the rubber seal of the inner lids inverted* so that the jars will not seal during sterilization (fig. 26).

Now the jars containing the rye can be sterilized. Add water to the pressure cooker; never use less than 1 to 1½ liters. Place the jars in the cooker, *making sure that the lids are loose* (fig. 28). If one's pressure cooker is large enough to permit, jars can be stacked in two tiers without difficulty (figs. 29 & 30). Seal the lid of the pressure cooker, but leave the stopcock open as before, until a head of steam begins to vent from the stopcock. Then close the stopcock, and bring to 15-20 lbs. pressure. Reduce heat when this pressure is reached so that pressure is maintained but does not increase. This is about medium heat on an electric stove. Sterilize at this pressure for one hour. Remove from the heat and allow the pressure to return to zero before opening the stopcock. Remember to wrap the stopcock column with a strip of Lysol-soaked paper toweling. Open the stopcock and allow excess steam to escape; then remove the lid from the pressure cooker. Remove one of the jars, tighten the lid down finger-tight, and carefully examine the jar for cracks and immediately discard any flawed jars (fig. 31); then shake the remaining jars vigorously (fig. 31). One can inscribe the jars with the date of inoculation or other suitable code-number (fig. 32) in order to keep track of the schedule of shaking the jars. One will note on removing the jar that the rye has absorbed the water and swelled to several times its previous volume. After shaking, leave the lids tightened until the jars have cooled. Place the jars into the pre-sterilized inoculating hood (if available) or onto the clean, disinfected working surface (fig. 10). Then let the jars cool for at least two hours or to room temperature.

When the jars have cooled completely to room temperature, and are no longer warm to the touch, they are ready to be inoculated. This step is best accomplished using a sterilized #11 scalpel (fig. 33). These scalpels can be obtained from any medical supply house. Flame the blades of the scalpel over an alcohol lamp (fig. 33). Insert the scalpel into an agar mycelial culture grown in a petri plate or baby food jar, and cut a grid into the surface, so that small squares of agar of about 1-1.5 cm square are formed (fig. 34). One can get about 9-20 small squares of agar from a single four-inch petri dish in this way (fig. 35). Cultures grown in slant tubes are obviously unsuitable for this step, because of difficulty in removing squares of agar from the tubes. At each transfer re-sterilize the scalpel blade by flaming, insert into the agar culture, and spear and remove one of the squares of mycelium-covered agar (fig. 36) and transfer rapidly to one of the Mason jars, lifting the lid of the jar just enough to insert the inoculum (figs. 37 & 38). Firmly tighten the lid and shake the jar vigorously to spread the inoculation points. Repeat this inoculation step for each jar.

An alternative method of inoculation was suggested to us by a friend, as possibly effective in increasing the sterility of the procedure and thus cutting down contamination. This method is a standard approach to fungal inoculations in mycological work, and so far seems promising, although we have not investigated it thoroughly enough to know if it is the answer to contamination problems.

fig. 17: Making a box: cutting a window in the lid.

fig. 18: Applying silicone marine glue.

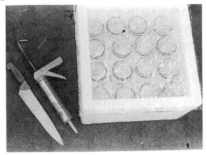

fig. 19: Clear plastic vinyl is glued over the window.

fig. 20: Completed box.

fig. 21: A set of jars to be filled and sterilized.

fig. 22: Materials for making the rye medium.

fig. 23: Adding weighed rye to the jar.

fig. 24: Two grams of powdered oyster shell ($CaCO_3$) are added.

fig. 25: 150 milliliters of water are added.

fig. 26: Mason jar lid with rubber edge up.

fig. 27: The All American 941½ pressure cooker.

fig. 28: Loading the pressure cooker.

fig. 29: The first layer of jars.

fig. 30: The second layer of jars.

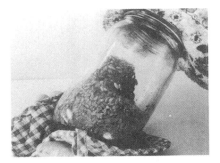

fig. 31: Sterilized jars are checked for cracks, then shaken.

fig. 32: Writing the date on the jars.

fig. 33: Flaming the scalpel.

fig. 34: Mycelium on agar is cut into sections.

fig. 35: Plate of sections ready for use.

fig. 36: Agar block is speared with scalpel...

fig. 37: ...and transferred...

fig. 38: ...to a jar.

fig. 39: Jars at 4, 6, and 10 days after inoculation.

In order to use this method, one must bore an approximately ½-in. diameter hole in the "dome" part of the dome-and-band Mason jar lids. One can easily have this done for a small fee at a machine shop which has a drill press. NOTE: Have the holes bored with the white side of the dome facing up! Seal the hole in the lid with a small piece of masking tape that has been folded back on itself at one end so it can be easily grasped. Sterilize the rye in the Mason jars in the manner described in the preceding pages. After the jars have been sterilized, sterilize the following items for 45 minutes in the pressure cooker: one 50 ml Pyrex pipette (wrapped in tinfoil); the *glass part* of a standard household blender; one 250 ml Erlenmeyer flask containing 100 ml of water (seal the top with tinfoil). The blender should be covered with tinfoil on top; *do not* sterilize the plastic top of the blender! The metal propeller and rubber gasket of the blender need not be removed, as they will not be harmed by high temperatures. After these items have been sterilized and the jars have cooled enough to inoculate, proceed as follows: Select one or two vigorous, uncontaminated mycelial cultures from your stock of inocula. Using the flat of a flamed kitchen knife, cut around the edges of the agar disk in the plate, and empty the disk or disks into the blender. Add 100 ml of sterilized water, place the top on the blender and homogenize at high speed for 20 to 30 seconds. Suck up the homogenate in the sterile pipette. Grasp the free end of the masking tape covering the hole in the lid of the jar. Place the tip of the pipette in the hole and allow 5 to 10 ml of homogenate to fall into the jar. Reseal the hole by re-sticking the tape. Repeat for each jar.

After the rye has been inoculated, a period of waiting and careful observation follows. The jars should be maintained at a roughly constant temperature of 70-80 degrees F., and 95% relative humidity. Since the lids remain on the jars the humidity will tend to be high and need not be worried about. Maintaining the relatively high and constant temperature, however, is important to promote early and rapid mycelial growth. The mycelium gives off heat as it grows and a styrofoam box of the sort used by tropical fish wholesalers is ideal for holding this heat and thus self-incubating the jars. During the first three days after inoculation, the mycelium will grow off the agar inoculum and onto the rye. By the eighth to fourteenth day, depending on the temperature, the mycelium will have grown radially outward from the inoculum in all directions to form a mat of growth slightly smaller than a fifty-cent piece.

When mycelial growth has reached this stage, firmly tighten the lid and again shake the culture vigorously, to break up the mycelium and redistribute the inoculum throughout the rye. During the shaking process you will run across obviously contaminated jars; simply remove them and set them aside for washing out later. After shaking, allow the culture to stand for 3-4 days. At the end of this time mycelial growth from many different points in the rye should be apparent (fig. 39). Shake the jars in this manner on the fourth, sixth, eighth, and, if necessary, on the tenth days after inoculation. Complete permeation of the rye should be observed anywhere from the eighth to the fourteenth day. At this time, the rye should be completely permeated by the snow-white mycelium, which may occasionally be lightly tinged with blue. If growth of any other color is observed, or if the rye is only partially permeated, then the culture is contaminated and should be discarded.

It should be noted that the time required for the mycelium to completely permeate the rye can vary widely according to individual circumstances. In some cases, permeation can take place in under eight days; in others, up to three weeks may be required. Our observations indicate that temperature of incubation of the jars is the single most critical factor governing permeation time. The mycelium of *Stropharia cubensis* has a growth optimum at about 80 degrees F. (Ames, 1958). We have found that cultures incubated at 80 degrees completed permeation in 11 to 13 days, while cultures incubated at 70 degrees required up to twice as long to complete permeation. A temperature of 68-70 degrees F. was, however, optimal for fruiting cultures after the casing step was carried out (see below). The degree of wetness of the rye medium also influenced permeation time, being slowed when the rye was too dry. We have found the best combination of rye and water to be approximately 160 ml rye to 130 ml water. We found these two factors, temperature and moisture, to affect permeation time significantly, while little discernable effect could be attributed to pH or the presence or absence of light. Even under optimum conditions, however, it is still necessary to shake the jars periodically to spread the inoculum through the medium and facilitate aeration. For the same reason one may also wish to loosen the lids of the jars (just a crack!) after the last shake.

When one or more jars of rye have been completely permeated by mycelium, the third step in the procedure is completed and one is ready to move on to the fourth step, casing. Before discussing this step, however, it is perhaps advisable to insert a word of caution with respect to the third step. This step, getting the mycelium to grow out and permeate the rye, seems to be the most difficult and discouraging step in the whole procedure. The peculiar headaches that one is faced with in this step can be summed up in one word: contamination. For some reason, contamination seems to be a much more serious problem at this stage than at the stage of growing on agar, probably because whole-grain rye is much more difficult to sterilize completely than is agar. Anyone attempting this step, in fact, is almost sure to receive a real education in the number of fungal and bacterial "weeds" that exist to plague the amateur mycologist. Our experience has been that two contaminants in particular are quite persistent and seemingly impossible to eliminate entirely. One is a crusty, rapidly-growing blue-green mold with a medicinal odor, probably a *Penicillium* or *Aspergillus*. The other is an unidentified bacteria that exudes a yellowish slime onto the side of the jar and that smells strongly of rotten apples. Spores of both of these organisms must be so commonly present in nature that they manage to contaminate some of the cultures despite the most careful inoculation procedures. The mold shows up rapidly and can be quickly spotted. Any culture seen to have this contaminant can be considered a loss. The bacteria takes longer to become obvious but with practice one can learn to spot it within a few days after inoculation. A sure giveaway for presence of this contamination is to loosen the lid slightly and sniff at the crack: a strong yeasty or ferment-like odor indicates the presence of contamination. Uncontaminated cultures give off only a slight smell of cooked rye. Cultures contaminated with this organism are also almost impossible to salvage. The bacterium is anaerobic, that is, it can grow in the absence of oxygen. Our experience is that it seems indifferent to the presence or absence of oxygen, and grows in either situation. The mushroom mycelium is quite aerobic, in fact proper aeration is essential for its growth; therefore proper aeration can afford the fungus something of a competitive advantage against this organism.

Other contaminants will occasionally be seen, although not with the regularity of the two already mentioned. These may include black, olive green or sulphur-colored molds, and sometimes a dirty-grey, rapidly growing mold that is probably a *Rhizopus.*

Three factors seem central to achieving a very low (5%) rate of contamination:

1. It is very important to let a good head of steam build up in the presssure cooker. If you are using the All American 941½ cooker, then it should vent clearly visible jets of steam for three to five minutes before the valve is closed and pressure allowed to build. 1500 ml of water should be covering the bottom of the 941½ at all times during the cooking of jars.

2. *Lysol, while easily available, has serious drawbacks. It is highly flammable and if used in the presence of the alcohol lamp or any other open flame can explode. CAUTION: Mushroom growers have been severely burned in accidents involving Lysol.* Staphene is the commercial name of a strong water-based disinfectant that can be obtained from a scientific or medical supply house or ordered from the manufacturer, Vestal Labs, St. Louis, MO. Staphene cannot explode but should be treated with respect and handled with rubber gloves, as it is very toxic.

3. Petri dishes of inoculum should be used when the expanding circle of growing mycelium still retains at least a ¼ in. margin of undisturbed agar on all sides. Contaminants enter the dishes at the edges and most locate there. If inoculum is taken from "young" growth areas, very few even slightly contaminated dishes of inoculum enter the process of inoculating large batches of jars.

Jar Shifting: Once jars are cased it is important to check them for any possible contamination that may take hold in the casing soil itself. If a system of shelves is used, then each day the jars in the back of each row should be transferred to the front of the row. During the transfer, examine the jar for signs of contamination and excessive dryness or wetness. And mites. Done regularly, this process results in examination of all the jars every few days. Contamination can thus be caught in its early stages before it has a chance to spread. It is especially important to eliminate colonies of blue and green bacteria that are powdery.

Contaminants of any kind are not good and it is advisable to discard immediately any culture seen to be contaminated. Although the mycelium can co-exist with some of the slower-growing fungal contaminants, it is still best to discard any contaminated cultures in order to avoid spreading the plague. The cleaning of jars should be done as far away from the inoculation area as possible and should be done by someone who is not involved in making sterile inoculations. Jars that have been contaminated should be washed in a strong solution of Clorox and water before being reused. The best way to deal with contamination is to not allow it to become established in the first place, by being extremely meticulous about one's sterilization and inoculation procedures. Always make sure that the jars are sterilized with *wet* heat, not dry, by allowing a head of steam to build up in the pressure cooker before closing the stopcock. An inoculating hood, even if it is as simple as a cardboard box with clear plastic in one side, becomes almost indispensable at this stage. Always use sterile, uncontaminated agar cultures as the source of inoculation. Make sure that the working surface, and the inside of the inoculating hood, are thoroughly disinfected before inoculation.

The general working environment should also be kept as clean and dust-free as possible. One may wish to use an electrostatic air cleaner for this but it is not essential. Also make sure that hands and arms are clean before inoculating, and wear latex rubber gloves if possible. Spray your gloved hands with spray Lysol before reaching into the hood. *Careful! Remember spray Lysol is flammable.* Use a sterilized scalpel for making inoculations, and be certain that it is absolutely clean for each batch to be inoculated. It does not hurt to swab it with alcohol beforehand. Be certain to flame the implement thoroughly in an alcohol flame before making each transfer. Practice making transfers as rapidly as possible, so that neither the receptacle containing the inoculum, nor the Mason jar are kept open longer than necessary. Finally, be absolutely ruthless in discarding contaminated cultures. Nothing less than complete permeation of the rye by the snow-white mycelium should be considered acceptable. If these procedures are followed rigorously, some cultures will undoubtedly still succumb to contamination, but the number can be held to a minimum.

STEP IV:
CASING AND RECASING

When one or more jars have been completely permeated by mycelium, one can move on to the fourth step in the process that leads directly to the production of mushrooms. In commercial mushroom culture, this step is called *casing*. In the method outlined here, casing consists of removing the dome and band lid of the jar, and covering the surface of the permeated rye with about ½ to ¾ in. (½ cup for quart jars) of sterilized soil (fig. 40 & 41). The soil should be premoistened to field capacity before being applied. The fastest way to do this is to spread the soil on a clean sheet of plastic and spray it lightly with the spray nozzle of a garden hose. Mix thoroughly. Field capacity can be gauged by the following rule of thumb: spray the casing soil just enough so that the soil is moistened throughout, but no water passes through the soil into the mycelium. In other words, moisten thoroughly, *but do not saturate* the soil. If the soil is to be sterilized, it should be moistened first. After sterilization, it can be conveniently stored in a double layer of plastic garbage bags, after it has cooled. Small amounts of casing soil may be dampened by putting two or three liters of casing soil in a large mixing bowl and moistening it with a pump sprayer. A large wooden spoon is perfect for folding the wet layers of soil into the dry. Alternate spraying the soil and stirring the dampness throughout the mix. When the casing soil has uniformly darkened in color and retains a shape when squeezed, it is ready to use. Once in the jar the soil should be shaken level and wetted a bit more with a fine mist sprayer (fig. 42 & 43). A fine-mist spray must be used to avoid sealing the surface of the casing soil.

After applying and moistening the casing soil, discard the lids and maintain the cultures in a high humidity environment. A large styrofoam cooler with a window cut into the lid and covered with clear or translucent polyethylene is excellent for this (fig. 17-20), so is a glass aquarium. If maintaining the jars in aquaria or styrofoam boxes, it is important to pay attention to proper aeration. Experience has shown that the daily transpiration/evaporation cycle is important if one is to have vigorous fruiting, healthy cultures. Maintaining the proper moisture balance and evaporation rate in the casing soil is actually a complex interplay among temperature, aeration, and evaporation. If either temperature or aeration is excessive, the soil will dry out. On the other hand, it should not become waterlogged, and a minimal amount of air movement should be present to facilitate a slow, even rate of evaporation from the casing soil. For this reason we recommend incubating the boxes with the lids partially or wholly removed after fruiting has begun. The temperature should be kept above 70 degrees F. Spray the cultures daily with a fine-mist spray just enough to make up for moisture lost through evaporation (fig. 44). Each cased jar requires 2-3 good squirts of water per day to maintain continuous fruiting. Do not exceed field capacity. A good test for proper moisture content is that the surface of the soil should feel moist and spongy to the touch. Boxes of newly cased jars should be stored in chronological order.

Watering becomes a critical matter at this stage. If the correct water level is maintained in the casing soil, the first flush of mushrooms will be normal. But if jars are allowed to become too dry, then aborted fruiting or formation of many small mushrooms unable to grow to full maturity will occur. With proper watering and proper aeration, perfectly normal first flushes can be grown. What is a proper amount of moisture? The general tendency seems to be for beginning cultivators to keep jars too dry. Remember always to use premoistened casing soil. Make sure the distribution of the moisture is uniform. Once jars have been cased with pre-dampened soil, they ordinarily only need water once a day. The exceptions occur during and after periods of intense fruiting when slightly more water is required, or during spells of dry, hot weather. Strong drafts, especially warm drafts from floor heaters, can dry jars out very quickly. If one keeps jars on shelves that are open to the surrounding room part of the day, then it is especially important to keep the heaters from blowing directly on jars. Shelves can be enclosed in transparent polyurethane film in order to maintain high humidity and minimize contamination.

The other extreme to avoid is overwatering. The casing layer should be kept damp but not soaked. Any visible water accumulating between the rye covered mycelium and the walls of the jar indicates overwatering and a potential for contamination. Often if left unattended such jars become yellowish, indicating a more advanced

fig. 40: Open jar and soil ready for casing.

fig. 41: ½ cup casing soil is applied.

fig. 42: Casing soil is shaken to even it . . .

fig. 43: . . . then sprayed, using a fine mist.

fig. 45: The mycelium grows through the casing soil.

fig. 47: 25 days after casing, the first mushrooms appear.

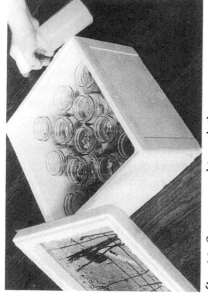

fig. 44: Spray cased jars daily.

fig. 46: Mycelium will also grow on the surface.

stage of contamination. Such jars should be placed on a shelf together—separate from the other jars—and *all water should be withheld* until excess water in the jars recedes completely. Often, upon recasing, such jars seem to regain their equilibrium, and fruiting, though delayed, is normal.

During the next two to three weeks, the mycelium will begin to grow up into the casing soil, penetrating it to just beneath the surface (fig. 45). The mycelium may occasionally break out onto the top of the soil and begin to spread across its surface, and part of the purpose of spraying daily is to keep this surface growth "knocked down" with the spray (fig. 46). Excessive surface growth, in which the mycelium completely overgrows the casing soil and forms a thick spongy crust on the surface, is an indication that the mycelium is starved for air and that ventilation should immediately be increased. If you are under-watering your jars, this surface mycelium will turn blue with thirst. As the mycelium grows into the casing soil, it will begin to form a network of ropy strands visible at the interface of the soil and the glass. This network gradually gains more and more intersecting nodes, and by the 14th to 20th day after casing, these nodes have differentiated into tiny white dots distributed through the casing soil along the perimeter of the jar. These dots are the young mushroom primordia; gradually they enlarge and incorporate more mycelia, slowing taking on the appearance of tiny mushrooms with squat, fat stems and dark, brownish heads. This is the "pin" stage in the development of the mushroom and the primordia at this stage are about 1-2 mm in length. These pins continue to enlarge and some will begin to thrust above the surface of the casing soil, both at the sides and in the center of the jar. Once the young mushrooms have penetrated the surface of the casing soil, another five to ten days is required for them to reach full maturity. At maturity the mushrooms may be 2 to 9 inches tall and have caps ranging from 1 to 3 inches in diameter (fig. 47 & 48). We have also found that these mushrooms do respond favorably to light, and that a daily 13-hour fluorescent or Grow-lux cycle results in mushrooms with larger caps and shorter stems than those grown without any special lighting. Probably it is not advisable, however, to place the cultures in direct sunlight for prolonged periods. While many mushrooms will grow to full size, approximately an equal number will grow to about half-size or less and then cease to grow; these "aborts" can still be plucked, dried, and used, although they are not as aesthetically appealing as the fully matured specimens. With practice one can learn to spot aborts early and remove them from the cultures. Aborted mushrooms left in the cultures are susceptible to attack by bacteria which quickly render them both ugly and unusable.

Excessive numbers of aborts are another indication of inadequate aeration. If the jars are being incubated in styrofoam boxes or aquaria, there is a possibility of accumulating carbon dioxide in the air space above the casing soil. This will inhibit fruiting and/or prevent fruits from reaching maturity. If this happens, increase aeration by leaving the lids off the box, or by using a small fan to enhance air movement over the surface of the jar. Be careful not to *over* aereate, however; too fast a rate of evaporation will cause the casing soil to dry out.

Occasionally mushroom primordia will form down toward the bottom of the jar and grow to maturity but will not break the surface of the casing soil. It is possible to inhibit this effect somewhat by wrapping jars with tinfoil to the top of the casing soil (fig. 45). This effect, formation and development of primordia toward the bottom of the jar, is normally seen during the earliest mushroom "flush." After the first flush, the jars are recased for each subsequent flush (see below). We find that recasing will largely eliminate this problem for all flushes but the first one.

A variety of types of casing soils have been found to effectively promote fruiting. We have found the following mixture to be one of the best:

7.5 liters peat moss
3.5 liters fine vermiculite
4 liters washed fine sand
2 liters calcium carbonate (finely crushed oyster shell)

Powdered oyster shell is sold as a feed supplement by many feed companies. The calcium carbonate is an optional ingredient and can be left out without significantly affecting fruiting. It should be added if available, however, to buffer the soil and keep it from becoming too acidic. This factor *may* contribute to the growth of contaminants on the surface of the casing soil, and the calcium carbonate can inhibit or prevent this. For the same reason, one may also wish to water occasionally using a saturated solution of calcium carbonate. We have also found that a mixture of one part mica-peat (50/50 vermiculite-peatmoss mixture) to one part potting soil will work.

Sterilization of casing soil is usually recommended but we found it unnecessary when relatively sterile commercially bagged materials were used. If you wish you may sterilize casing soil before use at 15-20 lbs. pressure for 30 minutes. It should be wetted first to field capacity. Casing soil can be stored indefinitely in a tightly sealed large glass jar, or in a polyethylene garbage bag. If a glass jar is used, it can be sterilized with the casing soil in it. Remember to loosen the lid prior to sterilizing. After the first flush of mushrooms, the soil and mycelium-covered block of grain will shrink somewhat, leaving a space between the mycelium and the walls of the jar. Whenever this condition is noticed, it is time to recase. Recasing will greatly extend the life and fruiting capacity of your jars. It is a simple procedure which involves using a clean fork (one per jar, as this way contaminants are not spread from jar to jar) to scrape off all of the old casing soil and aborted mushrooms growing down along the sides of the jar. Then, using fresh casing soil prewetted as before, recover the mycelial block and use the fork to work the fresh casing soil down the sides of the jar around the block as well as covering the top. It will take your jars about two weeks to recover from this treatment but then they will do their best fruiting, producing clusters of large carpophores and behaving as if this recasing procedure had made them more resistant to contamination.

Instead of applying the casing soil to the mycelia-covered rye in the jars as described in the preceding pages, it is possible to adopt a somewhat different approach to the making of cased cultures. The steps involved in this method are described briefly below. The basic idea for this method was suggested to us by a friend, Paul Kroeger, and his contribution is gratefully acknowledged. In order to use this method, one begins by growing the mycelium out on the rye in the Mason jars in exactly the manner described above for the cased jar method. One may use plastic trays, glass baking pans, or one may manufacture a styrofoam box with a window of clear plastic in the lid as described above (fig. 17-20). Sterilize the inside surface of the tray or box thoroughly by wiping down with a 25% Clorox solution followed by a Lysol spray. Cover the bottom of the container with a ¾-1 inch-deep layer of perlite or a 1:1 mixture of vermiculite and casing soil. Grow the mycelium on the rye medium in the Mason jars until it is fully permeated and ready to case. Instead of casing at this stage, however, shake the jars again. The mycelial block will be tightly woven together and may require a little extra effort in order to be shaken loose. After shaking, empty the contents of several jars into the container so as to form a layer of rye "spawn" about 1-1½ inch deep.

The number of jars required to do this will vary depending on the size of the container, but usually between five and ten jars are sufficient. Cover the rye layer with a second layer of moistened casing soil, to a depth of 1-1½ in. One has now created a 3-layered "sandwich" arrangement in the container: Perlite or vermiculite-casing soil forms the bottom layer and provides drainage; the second, rye and mycelium layer provides the nutritive substrate for the mycelium; the topmost, casing layer prevents the mycelium from becoming desicated or attacked by contaminants as well as functioning to induce the mycelium to fruit. Once the layers have been made, maintain the container in a humid environment and as close to 70 degrees F. as possible. If using styrofoam boxes, keep the lid on for the first two weeks following casing. Since the soil is moist and the mycelium produces water in its respiration, humidity will be high in the box (in fact, condensation on the transparent lid can usually be seen) and therefore one should not spray, or should spray only lightly and infrequently, during this stage.

Two weeks after casing, or approximately one week prior to the commencement of fruiting, the lids should be removed to prevent carbon dioxide accumulation in the containers. Daily watering with a fine mist can be started after the lids have been removed. The mycelium will continue to grow into the casing soil. Fruiting, at both the sides and center of the container, will commence 21-30 days after casing. The box or tray culture will fruit abundantly, producing many clusters of perfect large carpophores in various stages of maturity across the entire surface of the casing soil. As these clusters are plucked, the holes created in the casing soil should be plugged with fresh casing soil. Recasing as described for the jars is not necessary with this method. The container cultures will usually succumb to contamination (usually a green mold which shows up on the surface of the casing soil) more quickly than the jars. Containers fruit for 30 to 40 days as opposed to 60 to 80 days for jars, but the flushes produced during this time are so abundant that the overall total yield for trays and jars is comparable (approximately 10 grams dry weight of mushroom for every 100 grams dry weight of rye).

When your cultures are well established in the mature fruiting phase, it is a good idea to shift your awareness toward a new class of potential pests and carriers of contamination. These are insects, specifically flies and mites. The best way of controlling flies is by keeping your cultures in a screened room that flies are unable to penetrate. Even in the most tightly sealed environments flies do occasionally occur. It is therefore a good idea to use a slow acting insect killer of the vaporizing type, such as the "No-Pest Strip" in the growing area. Usually this is all the fly protection that is necessary. Mites are a more persistent and difficult pest to control. Massive reliance on applied insecticides is the commercial mushroom growers' approach to mite control. But we believe that application of insecticides to *Stropharia cubensis* should be undertaken only as a last resort.

The real key to mite control is early detection. Therefore, examine your jars very carefully. Mites are most visibly active in the middle and late afternoon, and are usually first spotted wandering around on the smooth rim of the jar. They are tiny specks, distinguished from tiny bits of casing material only by their motion. Jars with mites should be immediately isolated, or preferably removed entirely from the growing area. Once mites are detected, the grower must go to a state of high alert and check the jars every day to see if the plague is spreading. Removal of infested jars is the best course. The next best course is to spray only the infested jars with a ½-strength solution of Malathion. Malathion, though anathema to the anti-insecticide purist, is one of the least toxic and most rapidly degraded of commercial insecticides. It should not, however, be used on cultures within 6 days of fruiting. Under no conditions should the miticide Keldane be applied to cultures. Keldane is FATAL to *Stropharia cubensis*.

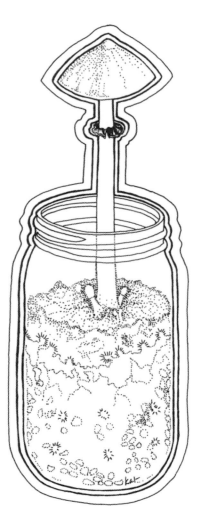

STEP V:
HARVESTING, PRESERVING, AND DOSAGE

As the mushroom matures to full size, the cap will enlarge and become more globular in shape. The gills will at first be covered by a flap of tissue, called the *veil*, that connects the margin of the cap with the stipe. As the cap enlarges, this veil will detach from the cap margin to form an *annulus*, or ring of ruptured veil tissue, on the stem. The mushroom can be harvested as soon as the veil rupture has occurred. If a spore print is to be collected, however, the mushroom should be allowed to flatten out to an umbrella shape before harvesting.

Freshly harvested mushrooms can be eaten fresh, or can be dried and sealed in plastic bags for preservation. It is a simple matter to construct a small drying cabinet out of masonite or plywood. This consists essentially of a wooden box with a hinged door on the front and two or more screens or wire shelves which can slide in and out. A 150- to 200-watt electric light bulb can be mounted in the bottom as a heat source. We have found this type of drying cabinet completely suitable and trouble-free. It produces an even heat at about 120 degrees F. and will dry even large, thick-stemmed mushrooms completely within 48 hours; smaller mushrooms dry in 24 hours using this cabinet. They may be dried in a gas oven at low heat (140 F. or less) for 6-10 hours (fig. 49 & 50). They may also be dried under a heat lamp, on a screen over a heating vent, or in a small electric food dehydrator. Mushrooms are fully dried when hard to the touch, like crackers, with no spongy feel at all (fig. 51).

Mushrooms that have been dried at too high a heat will turn brown and be very bitter to the taste. Such mushrooms are substantially less psychoactive. To preserve maximum potency, dried mushrooms should be sealed in five gram increments in plastic bags from which the air has been withdrawn (figs. 52-54), and this in turn placed in a tightly sealed glass vessel or other moisture-proof container, and frozen. We have found the polypropylene boiling bags used in food storage and preparation to be excellent for preserving dried mushrooms. Rolls of bagging material and the electric sealers used for sealing are sold commercially in department stores under the brand name

"Seal-A-Meal" and "Seal & Save." Dried mushrooms left in the open air quickly lose their potency. Fresh mushrooms should not be frozen without drying first, as freezing them in this condition will turn them into a black, gooey mess. Fresh mushrooms can, however, be preserved in a plastic bag in the vegetable pan of the refrigerator for about a week to ten days. Fresh mushrooms older than this should either be eaten or dried to prevent spoilage.

The dried mushrooms contain from 0.2 to 0.4 percent psilocybin (Schultes, et al., 1973) by weight. Some strains of *Stropharia cubensis* have been reported to contain as much as 0.5% psilocybin (Wasson & Heim, 1959, p. 260). Psilocin is present only in trace amounts. A dose of about 10-12 milligrams of psilocybin, or about 5 g dry weight of mushrooms, or 50 g wet weight, is sufficient to manifest the full spectrum of hallucinogenic effects in a 160 lb. adult. These effects include visual and auditory hallucinations, extreme hilarity, distortions of time and space perception, and a sense of emotional detachment from the environment. Less marked effects can be detected at doses as low as 2 mg, which is about 1-2 dried mushrooms. Fresh mushrooms seem to be somewhat stronger than dried ones. Psilocybin is one of the least toxic of all hallucinogens. A full, effective dose is 12 mg while mescaline, by comparison, has a minimum effective dose of 200 mg for an average-size adult, and a toxicity 2.5 times that of psilocybin (Aboul-Enein, 1974).

The state of mind induced by a full dose of mushrooms is one of euphoria and calm lucidity, with no loss of coherency or clarity of thought. The hallucinations seen with the eyes closed are colorful, hard-edged, and highly articulated, and may range from abstract geometrical forms to visions of fantastic landscapes and architectural vistas. These hallucinations are most intense when the mushroom is taken in the setting preferred by the Mazatecans: inside at night in complete darkness. On the other hand, if one is in a natural setting and directs the focus of the senses outward to the environment, one discovers that one's senses seem keyed to their highest pitch of receptivity, and finds oneself hearing, smelling and seeing things with a clarity and sensitivity seldom, if ever, experienced before. Although it should be clear to anyone who has read this far that cultivating these mushrooms is an endeavor requiring time, patience, care and humility, and one fraught with its own peculiar problems, once one has partaken of these wonderful gifts of nature and experiences the exalted consciousness that they can bring about, we think that they will agree with us that the effort involved provides its own ample reward.

fig. 48: Grasp the stalks firmly when harvesting.

fig. 49: Remove the soil from the bottoms of the stems.

fig. 50: Mushrooms ready for oven-drying.

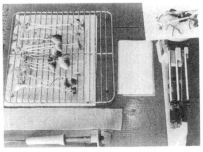

fig. 51: The dried mushrooms are weighed.

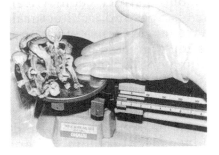

fig. 52: They are placed in plastic bags.

fig. 53: Bags are heat-sealed with a bag sealer.

fig. 54: Fresh mushrooms and dried ones ready for freezing.

AFTERWORD

Approximately sixty days after you began the isolation of spores, the first harvest will be possible from your rye-filled jars. Mushroom growing is like alchemy in that there is a division of the work into practical effort and visionary reward. The organic psilocybin within the mushroom is quality controlled by the very stable and ancient genes of the Stropharia. You, as the propagator and spiritual friend of the mushroom, can form a deep relationship with the mycelial ally and again and again make far journeys into its visionary realms if you observe a few simple rules. Tolerance to psilocybin is easily acquired if trips are taken more often than once a week. If one does acquire a tolerance, it can be gone around by either upping the dose or by laying off for a couple of weeks to allow your body to recover its equilibrium. We recommend the latter course even though the toxicity of psilocybin is so low that raising the dose is a valid alternate course.

Now our little handbook closes. Advice from this point on can only come in generalities. Take the mushrooms that you have grown, take them in the darkness as the Indians of Mexico who have used them for centuries do. Smoke a lot of your favorite hash to synergize the behind-the-eyelids hallucinations and prolong them. Psilocybin is light shedding illumination on a landscape both within and without the mind and body of human beings and previously invisible to them. The exploration of this vast region by persons whose mental equipage is that of the modern West has only begun. Only a moment has passed since our culture has rediscovered, through the work of Wasson and others, the ancient and unplumbed relationship between the vision-causing mushrooms and our own strangely gifted species. You are a pioneer in a world whose future is undetermined and whose living organisms are full of singularities and surreal transforming promise.

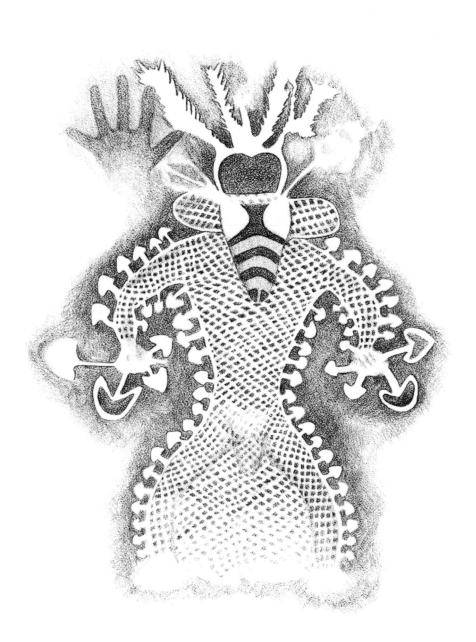

**Rock painting from Tassili Plateau,
Southern Algeria, circa 3500 B.C.**

CONVERSION TABLE

This conversion table is included for those who may lack scales or other equipment to make accurate measurements of required ingredients. Although one should always try to measure the ingredients as accurately as possible, and the purchase of an inexpensive scale and graduated cylinder is well worthwhile, this table can be useful in approximating measurements and calculating volumes if such equipment is unavailable.

160 ml dry rye weighs approximately 150 grams, $2/3$ of a cup

2 g powdered oyster shell is a level ½ teaspoon

1 g yeast extract is a level ½ teaspoon

1 g Difco agar is 1 slightly packed level ½ teaspoon

1 liter (1000 ml) = 1 quart (1.057 quarts)

1 baggy (Glad type) weighs 1.5 g

A CHRONOLOGY OF PSILOCYBIAN* MUSHROOMS
Compiled by Irimias the Obscure & O.T. Oss

c. 3500 B.C. Frescoes of dancing shamans holding mushrooms in the presence of white cattle are painted on the rock surfaces of the Tassili Plateau in Southern Algeria.**

c. 2500 B.C. Aryan people with hallucinogenic mushroom use as a central part of their religion enter India. Wasson has argued for *Amanita muscaria* as the identity of the mysterious Soma. The question remains an open one. A psilocybian mushroom may well have been the source of Soma.

c. 1100-400 B.C. Eleusinian Mystery rites using ergotized rye (Wasson) or psilocybian mushrooms (Graves) focus the mystical aspirations of the Ancient World.

300-500 B.C. In the latter half of this century, "mushroom stones" were found in highland Guatemala dating back at least as far as 300-500 B.C.

c. 300 A.D. Frescoes have been found in central Mexico with mushroom designs indicating the existence of a mushroom cult at this time.

387 A.D. St. Augustine, formerly a follower of Mani, condems Manichaeans for mushroom eating.

1502 A.D. Psilocybian mushrooms were served at the coronation feast of Moctezuma II and were used recreationally.

1547-1569 Fray Bernadino de Sahugun, A Spanish cleric, wrote *Historia de las Cosas de Nueva Espana* (also known as the *Florentine Codex*) which refers to "nanacatl" (= teonanácatl = flesh of the gods = psilocybian mushroom). Sahugun states that the mushrooms "are harmful and intoxicate like wine." Further, those who indulge "see visions, feel a faintness of heart and are provoked to lust."

1651 Dr. Francisco Hernández, a Spanish physician studying Central American Indian herbal medicine reported three types of mushrooms which were worshipped by Mexican natives. He reported that the ingestion of these caused "not death but a madness that on occasion is lasting, of which the symptom is a kind of uncontrolled laughter... these are deep yellow, acrid, and of a not displeasing freshness. There are others again, which without inducing laughter, bring before

---

* "Psilocybian" in this context means any mushroom containing psilocybin.

**Special thanks to J. Ginsberg of Boulder, Colorado who was the first to notice the importance of the Tasilli frescos for ethnomycology.

the eye all sorts of things, such as wars and the likeness of demons. Yet others there are not less desired by princes for their festivals and banquets, and these fetch a high price. With night-long vigils are they sought, awesome and terrifying. This kind is tawny and somewhat acrid."

1895   John Uri Lloyd publishes his fantasy-novel *Etidorpha* in which he makes it clear that he and his mycologist brother Curtis Gates Lloyd were aware of the hallucinatory properties of mushrooms other than *Amanita muscaria*. The Lloyds elected not to publish the botanical details of their findings.

1906   *Stropharia cubensis* is described by Earle in a Cuban agronomy journal.

1914   A.E. Merrill of Yale University published a paper in *Science* describing the hallucinogenic effects of ingesting *Panaeolus papilionaceus* from Oxford County, Maine. Although the identification of the mushroom may be in error, the effects described are very probably due to psilocybin and psilocin. Further, the article describes different reactions to this hallucinogenic mushroom which is compared to hashish and peyote in the text.

1915   American botanist William E. Safford attempted to identify the teonanácatl of the Aztecs. He claimed that sacred mushrooms had never existed, and that the teonanácatl referred to by the 16th century Spanish chroniclers were actually dried peyotl buttons. Safford's theory was widely accepted by the scientific community for the next three decades.

1919   Dr. Blas P. Reko, who had carried out extensive anthropological and botanical work in Mexico for more than 25 years, published an article in a Mexican anthropological journal stating that nanácatl (= teonanácatl) was a hallucinogenic mushroom. However, some of Reko's earlier work had been in error and this report was discounted.

1923   In a letter to the U.S. National Museum, Dr. Reko stated that teonanácatl "is actually, as Sahugun states, a fungus which grows on dung heaps and which is still used under the same old name by the Indians of the Sierra Juarez in Oaxaca in their religious feasts."

1936   Victor A. Reko (B.P.'s brother) publishes *Magische Gifte*. In it, he wrongly suggests that teonanácatl might be a species of *Amanita*.

1936   Ing. Roberto J. Weitlaner obtained some teonanácatl in Oaxaca. He was the first white man in modern times to have done so. He sent the specimens to B.P. Reko, who sent them to Harvard, where they arrived in a decomposed state and thus escaped identification.

1938   Weitlaner's daughter, Irmgard, along with anthropologist Jean Basset Johnson and two others attended a mushroom rite in Huatla, Oaxaca. These were the first whites to attend a mushroom ceremony.

1938   Harvard botanist R.E. Schultes traveled to Oaxaca and obtained from native informants two specimens of two different genera: *Panaeolus campanulatus* var. *sphinctrinus*, and *Stropharia cubensis*. In his field notes, he described a third specimen: *Psilocybe caerulescens* var. *Mazatecorum*.

1952-53   R. Gorden Wasson and his wife Valentina became aware of the existence of a mushroom cult in central Mexico. This ambitious couple set out to prove the theory that religion came directly from the use of hallucinogenic plants. The Wassons traveled to Mexico and were guided by Ing. Roberto J. Weitlaner to the mountainous village of Huautla de Jiménez in Oaxaca.

1955   R.G. Wasson and Allan Richardson became the first two Americans to attend a mushroom ritual and ingest the mushrooms. The mushrooms were taken under the supervision of Maria Sabina, Mazatec curandera. By 1957, news of this ritual had reached the world through articles in several popular magazines and the Wasson's book, *Mushrooms, Russia, and History.*

1956   Wasson invited Roger Heim, a French mycologist, to Oaxaca to research the use of the sacred mushrooms. Heim identified fourteen species and several subspecies belonging to three genera, *Psilocybe, Stropharia,* and *Conocybe.* Several of these species were new to mycology, but had been utilized as hallucinogens by the natives for centuries.

1957   Mycologist Dr. Rolf Singer and two young Mexican botanists, M.A. Palacios and Gustón Guzmán, arrived in Oaxaca to do taxonomic work on the mushrooms.

1958   Dr. Albert Hofmann, a Sandoz chemist from Basel, Switzerland, isolated two active agents and named them psilocybin and psilocin after the genus *Psilocybe.*

1960   While vacationing in Cuernavaca, Mexico, Harvard psychologist Timothy Leary ate a dose of the mushrooms. Later, he wrote " . . . it was the classic visionary voyage and I came back a changed man . . . You are never the same after you've had that one flash glimpse down the cellular time tunnel. You are never the same after you've had the veil drawn."

1960 Dr. Leary and an associate, Dr. Richard Alpert, obtained a supply of synthetic psilocybin from Sandoz for use in an experiment with prisoners in Concord State Prison, Massachusetts. Initial results were very promising: prisoners released following an experience with psilocybin seemed less likely to be re-arrested and returned for parole violations than other parolees.

1960 Aldous Huxley ingested 10 mg psilocybin in a group under the supervision of Timothy Leary. Huxley "sat in contemplative calm throughout; occasionally produced relevant epigrams; reported the experience as an edifying philosophic experience."

c. 1965-66 Laws against the sale, manufacture, and possession of LSD, mescaline and psilocybin are passed by paranoid legislatures after being persuaded by a hysterical press. The New York State legislature deferred hearings on one bill to outlaw hallucinogens until after the law was voted on and passed!

1966 By this time, several illicit labs were set up to manufacture hallucinogenic drugs in response to the growing demand by users.

1967 Reacting to erroneous tales of massive chromosome damage produced by LSD use, users began to demand organic drugs such as psilocybin and mescaline. Compared to LSD, hallucinogens such as these are relatively expensive to manufacture. Many unscrupulous dealers sold LSD as psilocybin. Most of the tabbed or capsulated psilocybin on the street from 1966-75 was actually LSD, or LSD cut with PCP.

1970 *A Key to the North American Psilocybin Mushroom* was published by Leonard Enos in California. This poorly-illustrated but well-written guide instructed laypersons where, when and how they could obtain psilocybian mushrooms in nature. The book also contained instructions for cultivating mycelium on agar.

1971 Due to popular demand for organic drugs, unscrupulous dealers began lacing commercial mushrooms with LSD and selling them as psilocybian mushrooms. These spurious psilocybian mushrooms appeared on the street drug market as late as 1975 and can be differentiated from most psilocybian mushrooms in that they (a) don't blue, and (b) their effects last much longer than the 4 to 7 hours characteristic of psilocybin.

1975 The first living cultures of *Stropharia cubensis* were seen in limited numbers on the underground market.

1975 Oss and Oeric (in this volume) bravely risked ridicule to become the first to suggest the extraterrestrial origin of *Stropharia cubensis*.

1976 Technology developed by the authors (Oss & Oeric, 1976) is unleashed upon the world. The illicit hallucinogenic trade crumbles because of decentralization brought on by epidemic of home *Stropharia* cultivation. Invasion of North America by hallucinogenic mushrooms continues, leading shortly to metamorphosis of human beings into a symbiotic species.

1981 Over one hundred thousand copies of *Psilocybin: Magic Mushroom Grower's Guide* sold. Numerous imitations also flourish as an estimated five thousand North American mushroom growers work with love and dedication to make psilocybin *the* hallucinogen of choice in high-tech society.

1984 Heterodox Bengali Hindus announce identification of the Vedic intoxicant Soma as a psilocybian mushroom, *Stropharia cubensis.* A reform of Hinduism centered around recovery of the 6000-year-old Soma rite is begun.

BIBLIOGRAPHY

Aboul-Enein, Hassan Y. "Psilocybin: A Pharmacological Profile." *Am. J. Pharm.*, May-June, 1974: 91-95.

Ames, R.W. "The Influence of Temperature on Mycelial Growth of *Psilocybe, Panaeolus,* and *Copelandia.*" *Mycopath. et Mycol. Appl.* 9:268-274 (1958).

Benedict, R.G., V.E. Tyler, & R. Watling. "Blueing in *Conocybe, Psilocybe* and a *Stropharia* Species and the Detection of Psilocybin." *Lloydia* 30 (2): 150-157 (1967).

Bocks, S.M. "The Oxidation of Psilocin by p-Diphenol Oxidase (Laccase)." *Phytochemistry* 6: 629-31 (1967).

Catalfomo, P., & V.E. Tyler. "The Production of Psilocybin in Submerged Culture by *Psilocybe cubensis.*" *Lloydia* 27 (1): 53-63 (1984).

Chang, S.T. & W.A. Hayes, *The Biology and Cultivation of Edible Mushrooms.* Academic Press, New York, 1978.

Enos, Leonard. *A Key to the North American Psilocybin Mushroom.* Youniverse Productions, 1970.

Estrada, Alvero. *Maria Sabina: Her Life & Chants.* Ross-Erikson Inc., Santa Barbara, CA. 1981.

Graves, Robert. *Food for Centaurs,* Doubleday & Co., N.Y., 1957.

Lloyd, John Uri. *Etidorpha,* (1895), Amherst Press, 1985).

McKenna, Terence and Dennis. *The Invisible Landscape,* Seabury Press, 1976.

McKenna, Terence. *True Hallucinations* (talking book . Lux Natura, Berkeley, 1984.

Miller, Orson K. *Mushrooms of North America.* E.P. Dutton & Co., New York, 1972.

Munn, Henry. "The Mushrooms of Language" in *Hallucinogens and Shamanism,* ed. by Harner, Michael, Oxford Univ. Press, 1973.

Neal, J.M., R.G. Benedict, & L.R. Brady. "Interrelationship of Phosphate Nutrition, Nitrogen Metabolism, and Accumulation of Key Secondary Metabolates in Saprophytic Cultures of *Psilocybe cubensis, Psilocybe cyanescens,* and *Panaeolus campanulatus.*" *J. Pharmaceut. Sci.* 57: 1661-1667 (1968).

Pollock, Steven. "Psilocybin Mushroom Pandemic." *J. Psyched. Drugs* 7(1): 73-84 (1975).

San Antonio, J.P. "A Laboratory Method to Obtain Fruit from Cased Grain Spawn of the Cultivated Mushroom, *Agaricus bisporus.*" *Mycologia* 63: 16-21 (1971).

Scagel, R.F., G.E. Rouse, J.R. Stein, R.J. Bandoni, W.B. Scho-field & T.M.C. Taylor. *An Evolutionary Survey of the Plant Kingdom.* Wadsworth Publishing Co., Belmont, CA, 1965.

Schultes, R.E. & Albert Hofmann. *The Botany and Chemistry of Hallucinogens.* Charles C. Thomas, Springfield, IL, 1973.

Singer, R. "Mycological Investigations on Teonanacatl, the Mexican Hallucinogenic Mushroom, Pt. 1," *Mycologia* 50: 239-261 (1958).

Stamets, P., *Psilocybe Mushrooms and Their Allies,* Homestead Book Co., Seattle, WA, 1978.

Stamets, P. & J.S. Chilton, *The Mushroom Cultivator,* Agarikon Press, Olympia, WA, 1983.

Wasson, R.G. "Seeking the Magic Mushroom." *Life* magazine, May 13, 1957.

_____, & V.P. Wasson. *Mushrooms, Russia and History.* Pantheon Books, New York, 1957 (out of print).

_____. "The Divine Mushroom: Primitive Religion and Hallucinatory Agents." *Proc. Am. Phil. Soc.* 102(3). June 24, 1958.

_____. "The Hallucinogenic Mushrooms of Mexico: An Adventure in Ethnomycological Exploration." *Tans. NY Acad. Sci.,* Ser. II, 21(4), February 1959.

_____, & R. Heim. *Les Champignons Hallucinogenes du Mexique: Etudes Enthologiques, Taxinomiques, Biologiques, Physiologiques et Chimiques.* Museum National d'Historie Naturelle, Paris, 1959.

_____. *Soma: Divine Mushroom of Immortality,* Harcourt, Brace, Jovanovich, 1968.

_____. *Maria Sabina and Her Mazatec Mushroom Velada,* Harcourt, Brace, Jovanovich, New York, 1974.

_____, C. Ruck & A. Hofmann, *The Road to Eleusis,* Harcourt, Brace, Jovanovich, New York, 1978.

_____. *The Wondrous Mushroom,* McGraw-Hill, New York, 1980.

GLOSSARY

adnate (of gills)—attached directly to the stalk.

adnexed (of gills)—notched just at stalk.

aerobic—requiring oxygen in order to live. Opposite of anaerobic.

annulus—ring-shaped remains of the partial veil which hangs on the stalk.

basidium (pl. basidia)—cell on which the spores of a Basidiomycete are borne.

basidiocarp—basidium-bearing structure or "fruiting body" of a Basidiomycete. Sometimes also called a *carpophore*.

basidiospore—spore formed exogenously on a basidium, generally following karyogamy and meiosis.

dikaryotic—a fungal hypha having two nuclei per cell.

diploid—having a single set of paired chromosomes (twice the number of chromosomes as in the gametes); 2n. Cf. *haploid*, having only one full set of *unpaired* chromosomes; n.

genome—the basic set of chromosomes (n) contributed by each parent.

genus (pl. genera)—the major subdivision of a family or subfamily of plants or animals; it usually consists of more than one species.

heterothallic—in Basidiomycetes, having thalli separable into two or more morphologically similar sexual strains, with conjugation occurring only when compatible mating types are paired.

hypha (pl. hyphae)—one of the tubular filaments composing mycelium.

indole—a white crystalline compound, C_8H_2N, having the same heterocyclic fused ring structure as the amino acid tryptophane. The indole structure is incorporated into the structures of many hallucinogenic compounds.

inoculation—to implant microorganisms or fungal mycelium into a culture medium. The mycelium used for this is called the *inoculum* (pl. inocula).

inoculating loop—implement used for making inoculations, consisting of a long handle with a length of stainless steel or platinum wire attached to the end and usually bent into a loop at the tip.

karyogamy—fusion of the two nuclei of the dikaryotic mycelium. In the Basidiomycetes, karyogamy constitutes the only diploid (2n) stage in the life cycle.

meiosis—reduction division of a cell in which the number of chromosomes is reduced from the diploid (2n) to the haploid (n) state. Meiosis produces sexual cells or *gametes.*

milliliter (abbr. ml)—one-thousandth part of a liter. 1 ml = 1 cubic centimeter (cc) in volume.

monokaryotic—hyphal condition in which the cells contain a single haploid nucleus; e.g., the primary mycelium of Basidiomycetes.

mycelium (pl. mycelia)—the vegetative body of certain complex fungi, consisting of an aggregation of hyphae.

phylogeny—the evolutionary development of a species of plant or animal.

rhizoid—a rootlike filament composed of many strands of hyphae.

somatogamy—fusion of somatic (body) cells rather than differentiated sexual cells as in the Basidiomycetes; does not include karyogamy.

species—the major subdivision of a genus or subgenus; it is composed of related individuals that resemble each other and are able to breed among themselves but usually not with other species.

tetrapolar—condition referring to sexual compatibility of some Basidiomycetes in which two sets of factors are involved (such as A,a & B,b).

thallus (pl. thalli)—the undifferentiated body of the fungus; the mycelial mass.

veil—the *partial* veil is a covering that extends from the unopened margin of the mushroom cap to the stalk, and that ruptures to form the annulus; the *universal* veil is a tissue surrounding the entire developing mushroom, usually lost early in development. *Stropharia cubensis* has a partial and universal veil.